First World War
and Army of Occupation
War Diary
France, Belgium and Germany

42 DIVISION
125 Infantry Brigade
Lancashire Fusiliers
1/8th Battalion
1 March 1917 - 29 March 1919

WO95/2655/2

The Naval & Military Press Ltd
www.nmarchive.com
Published in association with The National Archives

Published by

The Naval & Military Press Ltd

Unit 10 Ridgewood Industrial Park,

Uckfield, East Sussex,

TN22 5QE England

Tel: +44 (0) 1825 749494

www.naval-military-press.com

www.nmarchive.com

This diary has been reprinted in facsimile from the original. Any imperfections are inevitably reproduced and the quality may fall short of modern type and cartographic standards.

© **Crown Copyright**
Images reproduced by permission of The National Archives, London, England, 2015.

Contents

Document type	Place/Title	Date From	Date To
Heading	WO95/2655/2 1/8 Lancashire Fusiliers-42 Div Mar 1917-Mar 1919		
Heading	42nd Division 125th Infy Bde 1-8th Bn Lancs Fus. Mar 1917-Mar 1919		
Heading	War Diary of 1st/8th Lancashire Fusiliers.		
War Diary	At Sea	01/03/1917	02/03/1917
War Diary	On Train	03/03/1917	04/03/1917
War Diary	Erondelle	05/03/1917	15/03/1917
War Diary	Hamel	16/03/1917	25/03/1917
War Diary	Feuillires	26/03/1917	31/03/1917
Heading	War Diary Of 1st/8th Lancashire Fusiliers 1.4.17 To 30.4.17 Volume 24		
War Diary	Feuilleres	01/04/1917	05/04/1917
War Diary	Peronne	06/04/1917	10/04/1917
War Diary	Longavesnes	11/04/1917	13/04/1917
War Diary	Saulcourt	14/04/1917	14/04/1917
War Diary	Cartigny	15/04/1917	17/04/1917
War Diary	Feuilleres	18/04/1917	21/04/1917
War Diary	Mons En Chaussee	22/04/1917	27/04/1917
War Diary	Peronne	28/04/1917	29/04/1917
War Diary	Doingt	30/04/1917	30/04/1917
Heading	War Diary Of 1st/8th Lancashire Fusiliers From 1st May 1917 To 31st May 1917 Volume 25		
War Diary	Doingt	01/05/1917	02/05/1917
War Diary	Tincourt	03/05/1917	03/05/1917
War Diary	St Emilie	04/05/1917	05/05/1917
War Diary	Saulcourt	06/05/1917	09/05/1917
War Diary	In The Line	09/05/1917	13/05/1917
War Diary	Peiziere	13/05/1917	17/05/1917
War Diary	In The Line	17/05/1917	19/05/1917
War Diary	Villers Faucon	20/05/1917	20/05/1917
War Diary	Equancourt	21/05/1917	23/05/1917
War Diary	In The Line	23/05/1917	26/05/1917
War Diary	Bertincourt	27/05/1917	31/05/1917
Heading	War Diary Of 1st/8th Lancashire Fusiliers From 1/6/17 To 30/6/17 Volume 26		
War Diary	Bertincourt	01/06/1917	04/06/1917
War Diary	In The Line	05/06/1917	16/06/1917
War Diary	Havrincourt Wood	17/06/1917	29/06/1917
War Diary	Ytres	30/06/1917	30/06/1917
Heading	War Diary 1st/8th Lancashire Fusiliers From 1/7/17 To 31/7/17 Volume 27		
War Diary	Ytres	01/07/1917	06/07/1917
War Diary	Gomiecourt	07/07/1917	31/07/1917
Heading	War Diary Of 7/8th Lancashire Fusiliers From 1st August 1917 To 31st August 1917 Volume 28		
War Diary	Gomiecourt	01/08/1917	20/08/1917
War Diary	Bouzincourt	21/08/1917	23/08/1917
War Diary	Belgium France 27 L 14 b 8.4	24/08/1917	27/08/1917
War Diary	Belgium 28 N.W.	28/08/1917	28/08/1917

War Diary	H.11	29/08/1917	29/08/1917
War Diary	I.5.a.1.7	30/08/1917	31/08/1917
Heading	War Diary Of 1/8th Lancashire Fusiliers From 1-9-17 To 30-9-17 Vol.29		
War Diary	Belgium 28 N.W.	01/09/1917	01/09/1917
War Diary	Sq.Farm C30.b.7.8	01/09/1917	07/09/1917
War Diary	Toronto Camp G 18 a.4.7	08/09/1917	13/09/1917
War Diary	Square Farm	14/09/1917	17/09/1917
War Diary	Ayr Camp G 10 d 9.3	18/09/1917	18/09/1917
War Diary	Jean-Ter Biezend L.3 Central	19/09/1917	21/09/1917
War Diary	Ledringhem	22/09/1917	23/09/1917
War Diary	Ghyvelde Shee 19 1/40.000	24/09/1917	24/09/1917
War Diary	St.Idesbald	25/09/1917	30/09/1917
Heading	War Diary Of 1st/8th Lancashire Fusiliers From 1/10/17 To 31/10/17 Volume 30		
War Diary	St Idesbald	01/10/1917	04/10/1917
War Diary	In The Line	05/10/1917	22/10/1917
War Diary	Coxyde	23/10/1917	29/10/1917
War Diary	La Panne	29/10/1917	31/10/1917
Heading	War Diary Of 1st/8th Lancashire Fusiliers From 1/11/17 To 30/11/17 Vol. 31		
War Diary	La Panne	01/11/1917	06/11/1917
War Diary	In The Line Batt HQ At M 27 b 70/65	07/11/1917	13/11/1917
War Diary	Batt. HQ M 27 b 70/65	14/11/1917	17/11/1917
War Diary	Canada Camp	18/11/1917	19/11/1917
War Diary	Esquelbecq	20/11/1917	20/11/1917
War Diary	Zermezeele	21/11/1917	21/11/1917
War Diary	Wallon Cappel Area	22/11/1917	22/11/1917
War Diary	Boeseghem	23/11/1917	26/11/1917
War Diary	Gorre and Quesnoy	27/11/1917	27/11/1917
War Diary	In The Line	28/11/1917	30/11/1917
Heading	War Diary Of 1st/8th Lancashire Fusiliers From 1/12/17 To 31/12/17 Volume 32		
War Diary	In The Line	01/12/1917	10/12/1917
War Diary	Oblinghem	11/12/1917	31/12/1917
Heading	War Diary Of 1/8th Lancashire Fusiliers From 1.1.18 To 31.1.18 Volume 33		
War Diary	Gorre	01/01/1918	02/01/1918
War Diary	Gorre & In The Line Festobert	03/01/1918	03/01/1918
War Diary	Festubert	03/01/1918	03/01/1918
War Diary	In The Line	04/01/1918	09/01/1918
War Diary	Givenchy	09/01/1918	17/01/1918
War Diary	Oblinghem	18/01/1918	28/01/1918
War Diary	Oblinghem & In The Line	29/01/1918	29/01/1918
War Diary	In The Line	30/01/1918	31/01/1918
Operation(al) Order(s)	Operation Orders No. 66	02/01/1918	02/01/1918
Operation(al) Order(s)	Administrative Instructions Issued In Conjunction With Operation Order No. 66	02/01/1918	02/01/1918
Operation(al) Order(s)	Operation Order No. 69	13/01/1918	13/01/1918
Operation(al) Order(s)	Administrative Instructions Issued In Conjunction With O.O. 69	13/01/1918	13/01/1918
Operation(al) Order(s)	Operation Order No. 69a.	25/01/1918	25/01/1918
Operation(al) Order(s)	Operation Order No. 70	27/01/1918	27/01/1918
Operation(al) Order(s)	Administrative Instructions Issued In Accordance With O.O.70	27/01/1918	27/01/1918
Operation(al) Order(s)	March Table To Accompany O.O. 70	27/01/1918	27/01/1918

Heading	War Diary Of 1/8th Lancashire Fusiliers From 1/2/18 To 28/2/18 Volume 34		
War Diary	In The Line	01/02/1918	02/02/1918
War Diary	La Bassee Canal Sector	01/02/1918	02/02/1918
War Diary	In Support	03/02/1918	07/02/1918
War Diary	In The Line	08/02/1918	14/02/1918
War Diary	Vaudricourt	15/02/1918	28/02/1918
Heading	42nd Division 125th Infantry Brigade 1/8th Battalion Lancashire Fusiliers March 1918		
Heading	War Diary Of 1/8th Lancashire Fusiliers From 1-3-18 To 31-3-18 Volume 35		
War Diary	Vaudricourt Ref. Map Bethune 1/40.000	01/03/1918	22/03/1918
War Diary	Ref Maps Bethune 1/40.000 Lens No. 11 1/100.000	23/03/1918	23/03/1918
War Diary	Sheet 57E N.W. 1/20.000	24/03/1918	24/03/1918
War Diary	Ref. Map Sheet 57E N.W. 1/20.000	25/03/1918	25/03/1918
War Diary	Sheet 57 N.E. 1/20.000	26/03/1918	31/03/1918
Heading	125th Inf. Bde. 42nd Div. 1/8th Battn. The Lancashire Fusiliers April 1918		
Heading	War Diary Of 1/8 Lancashire Fusiliers From 1.4.18 To 30.4.18 Volume 36		
War Diary	Sheet 57D. NE 1/20.000	01/04/1918	07/04/1918
War Diary	Lens Sheet 11 1/100000	08/04/1918	12/04/1918
War Diary	Sheet 67D 1/40000	13/04/1918	15/04/1918
War Diary	Sheet 57D 1/4000	16/04/1918	25/04/1918
War Diary	Sheet 57D N E 1/20000	26/04/1918	30/04/1918
Heading	War Diary Of 1/8th Lancashire Fusiliers From 1.5.18 To 31.5.18 Volume 37		
War Diary	Rossignol Farm 1/20000 57D.N.E.	01/05/1918	02/05/1918
War Diary	Ref 1/20000 57D NE K.6.A.2.2	03/05/1918	06/05/1918
War Diary	Couin Wood	07/05/1918	12/05/1918
War Diary	Couin Wood 57D.N.E. 1/30.000	13/05/1918	31/05/1918
Heading	War Diary Of 1/8th Lancashire Fusiliers From 1st 6.18. To 30th.6.18. Volume 38		
War Diary	Ref 57 D N E 1/20,000	01/06/1918	01/06/1918
War Diary	J.2.A.80.30. Couin Wood	02/06/1918	06/06/1918
War Diary	Sailly Au Bois	07/06/1918	15/06/1918
War Diary	Hebuterne	16/06/1918	23/06/1918
War Diary	Ref 57 D N E 1/20000. Hebuterne	23/06/1918	30/06/1918
Heading	War Diary Of 1/8 Lancashire Fusiliers From 1st.7.18. To 31st.7.18. Volume 39		
War Diary	Ref 57D N E 1/20000 Hebuterne	01/07/1918	02/07/1918
War Diary	Bivouacs J.22.C. & Purple Peserve	03/07/1918	10/07/1918
War Diary	Colincamps	11/07/1918	18/07/1918
War Diary	Ref 57 D N E SE 1/20000	18/07/1918	19/07/1918
War Diary	Q.1.B.0.5	26/07/1918	27/07/1918
War Diary	Bus-les-Artois Camp at J.20.A.8.0	28/07/1918	31/07/1918
Heading	War Diary Of 1/8th Lancashire Fusiliers From 1st.8.18 To 31st.8.18 Volume 40		
War Diary	Ref. 59 D N E & SE 1/20,000	01/08/1918	01/08/1918
War Diary	Bus-Les-Artois Camp at J 20 A.8.0	02/08/1918	03/08/1918
War Diary	K 19 C 6.0	04/08/1918	13/08/1918
War Diary	Ref. 57 D N E And SE	14/08/1918	20/08/1918
War Diary	Ref. 57 D.N.E 1/20,000 57 C	21/08/1918	26/08/1918
War Diary	Ref 57 C	27/08/1918	30/08/1918
War Diary	57 C N W	31/08/1918	31/08/1918
War Diary	57 C S W	31/08/1918	31/08/1918

Type	Description	Start	End
Heading	War Diary Of 1/8 Lancashire Fusiliers From 1/9/18 To 30/9/18 Volume 41		
War Diary	Ref Map Sheet 57 C 1/40000 Brick Fields Thilloy	01/09/1918	02/09/1918
War Diary	Riencourt	02/09/1918	03/09/1918
War Diary	Bus	03/09/1918	03/09/1918
War Diary	Ref Map Sheet 57c 1/40000 Bus	03/09/1918	04/09/1918
War Diary	Ytres	04/09/1918	05/09/1918
War Diary	Ref Map Sheet 57c 1/40000 Pys	06/09/1918	21/09/1918
War Diary	Le Bucquiere	22/09/1918	24/09/1918
War Diary	Ref Map Sheet 57 C 1/40000 LeBucquiere	25/09/1918	26/09/1918
War Diary	Trescault	27/09/1918	27/09/1918
War Diary	Ref Map Sheet 57 C 1/40000 Trescart	27/09/1918	29/09/1918
War Diary	Havrincourt Wood	30/09/1918	30/09/1918
Diagram etc	Appendix III Sheet 57c 1/40000		
Diagram etc	Sectional Diagram Appendix IV		
Diagram etc	Sectional Diagram Appendix V		
Diagram etc	Diagram Appendix VI		
Diagram etc	Sectional Showing C		
Heading	War Diary Of 1/8 Lancashire Fusiliers From 1/10/18 To 31/10/18. Volume 42		
War Diary	Ref Map Sheet 57 C B & 1/40000 Havrincourt Wood	01/10/1918	08/10/1918
War Diary	Villers Plouich	09/10/1918	09/10/1918
War Diary	Esnes	10/10/1918	10/10/1918
War Diary	Ref Map Sheet 57B 1/40000	10/10/1918	10/10/1918
War Diary	Fontaine-Au-Pire	11/10/1918	11/10/1918
War Diary	Herpigny Farm	12/10/1918	12/10/1918
War Diary	Viesly & Briastre	13/10/1918	14/10/1918
War Diary	Ref Map Sheet 57 B 1/40000 Viesly And Briastre	14/10/1918	15/10/1918
War Diary	D.26.A.9.2	16/10/1918	21/10/1918
War Diary	E 14.a.5.1	21/10/1918	21/10/1918
War Diary	Ref Map Sheet 57B 1/40000 S.E. Of Solesmes	21/10/1918	21/10/1918
War Diary	Sunken Road E.14.A.5.1	21/10/1918	23/10/1918
War Diary	Viesly	24/10/1918	24/10/1918
War Diary	Fontaine-Au-Pire	25/10/1918	26/10/1918
War Diary	Ref Map Sheet 57B 1/40000 Fontaine-Au-Pire	27/10/1918	31/10/1918
Operation(al) Order(s)	1/8th Lancashire Fusiliers. Operation Order No. 116	07/10/1918	07/10/1918
Operation(al) Order(s)	1/8th. Lancashire Fusiliers. Operation Order No. 118	11/10/1918	11/10/1918
Operation(al) Order(s)	1/8th Lancashire Fusiliers Operation Order No. 119	12/10/1918	12/10/1918
Heading	Rear O.R. File		
Miscellaneous	Head Quaiters 125 Infantry Bde.	14/10/1918	14/10/1918
Miscellaneous	Rear O.R. War Diary Gus		
Operation(al) Order(s)	1/8th Lancashire Fusiliers Operation Order No. 120	15/10/1918	15/10/1918
Operation(al) Order(s)	1/8th Lancashire Fusiliers Operation Orders No. 121	19/10/1918	19/10/1918
Operation(al) Order(s)	1/8th Lancashire Fusiliers Operation Order No. 122	21/10/1918	21/10/1918
Miscellaneous	Telegram		
Operation(al) Order(s)	1/8th Lancashire Fusiliers Order No. 123	22/10/1918	22/10/1918
Miscellaneous	Monu W.D.	23/10/1918	23/10/1918
Operation(al) Order(s)	1/8 Lancashire Fusiliers Order No 125	23/10/1918	23/10/1918
Miscellaneous	Headquarters 125th Inf Brigade.	23/10/1918	23/10/1918
Heading	War Diary Of 1/8 Lancashire Fusiliers From 1/11/18 To 30/11/18 Volume 43		
War Diary	Ref Map Sheet 57B 1/40000 Fontaine-Au-Pire	01/11/1918	04/11/1918
War Diary	Solesmes	05/11/1918	05/11/1918
War Diary	Ref Map Sheet 51A & 51 1/40000 Beaudignies R.32.bD	06/11/1918	06/11/1918
War Diary	Herbignies M 29 T 30	07/11/1918	07/11/1918

Type	Description	Date From	Date To
War Diary	La Haute Rue O.33.C.	08/11/1918	08/11/1918
War Diary	Ref Map Sheet 51 1/40000 P.33.A.8.4	08/11/1918	09/11/1918
War Diary	Hautmont	10/11/1918	15/11/1918
War Diary	Ref Map Sheet 51 1/40000 Hautmont	16/11/1918	30/11/1918
Operation(al) Order(s)	1/8th. Lancashire Fusiliers Operation Order No. 126	03/11/1918	03/11/1918
Miscellaneous	Secret.	04/11/1918	04/11/1918
Operation(al) Order(s)	1/8th. Lancashire Fusiliers Operation Order No. 127	05/11/1918	05/11/1918
Operation(al) Order(s)	1/8th. Lancashire Fusiliers Operation Order No. 128	06/11/1918	06/11/1918
Operation(al) Order(s)	1/8th. Lancashire Fusiliers Operation Order No 129	06/11/1918	06/11/1918
Operation(al) Order(s)	1/8th Lancashire Fusiliers Operation Orders No. 130	07/11/1918	07/11/1918
Operation(al) Order(s)	1/8th Lancashire Fusiliers Order No 131	25/11/1918	25/11/1918
Operation(al) Order(s)	1/8th Lancashire Fusiliers Order No. 132	29/11/1918	29/11/1918
Heading	War Diary Of 1/8 Lancashire Fusiliers From 1/12/18 To 31/12/18 Volume 44		
War Diary	Ref Map Sheet 51 1/40000 Hautmont	01/12/1918	14/12/1918
War Diary	Maubeuge (Namur 8) 1/100,000	15/12/1918	16/12/1918
War Diary	Estinne-Au-Mont	16/12/1918	16/12/1918
War Diary	Anderlues	17/12/1918	18/12/1918
War Diary	Charleroi	19/12/1918	19/12/1918
War Diary	Ref Map Namur 8 1/100,000 Charleroi	20/12/1918	31/01/1919
Heading	War Diary Of 1/8th Lancashire Fusiliers From 1/2/19 To 28/2/19 Volume 46		
War Diary	Ref Map Namur 1/100000 Charileroi	01/02/1919	29/03/1919
Miscellaneous	4 Copies		

WO95/2655 - 2

1/8 Lancashire Fusiliers - 42 Div

Mar 1917 - Mar 1919

42ND DIVISION
125TH INFY BDE

1-8TH BN LANCS FUS.

MAR 1917 - MAR 1919

42ND DIVISION
125TH INFY BDE

Vol. 2

H.N.
7 sheets

CONFIDENTIAL

WAR DIARY

of

1st/8th LANCASHIRE FUSILIERS.

From 1.3.17   To 31.3.17

Volume 23.

Mar 17
Mar 19

Army Form C. 2118.

WAR DIARY
or
INTELLIGENCE SUMMARY. 1/8th Lancashire Fusiliers
(Erase heading not required.)

Instructions regarding War Diaries and Intelligence Summaries are contained in F.S. Regs., Part II. and the Staff Manual respectively. Title pages will be prepared in manuscript.

Hour, Date, Place	Summary of Events and Information	Remarks and references to Appendices
AT SEA. MARCH. — 1st/2nd.	The ship (H.M.T. Transylvania) arrived in port at Marseilles France at 8.30 A.M. on the 2nd. The unit disembarked at 1 P.M. and entrained for Pont-Remy at 3.30 P.M. Strength of unit entraining :- officers 27 - other ranks 772.	R.J.J.
ON TRAIN. 3rd/4th. "	The journey took 53½ hours. There were 3 one-hour halts in every 24 for meals. On arrival at Pont-Remy station at 4th the unit detrained and marched to the village of Erondelle, a distance of one mile. Billeting of the unit was completed by mid-night.	Ref. Map. FRANCE. ABBEVILLE 14. Scale 1/100,000 K:6 R.J.J.
IRONDELLE. 5th/13th. "	In billets. Considering the severe nature of the weather these were very fine cases of sickness. Route-marching and musketry formed programme of work. 2Lt. N. Zimmern and 2Lt. H. Buckley rejoined from duty with 1/5th Lancashire Fusiliers on the 6th. 2Lt. J. Carter 1/5th Lancashire Fusiliers rejoined his own unit also on the 6th. 2nd Lt. I.Y. Harrison and 2nd Lt. L.H. Pettit joined the unit for duty from England on the 7th.	R.J.J.

WAR DIARY

INTELLIGENCE SUMMARY. 1/8th LANCASHIRE FUSILIERS

Army Form C. 2118.

Hour, Date, Place	Summary of Events and Information	Remarks and references to Appendices
ERONDELLE MARCH 5th/13th	2Lt N. ZIMMERN attached to 125th Bde H.Q. as intelligence officer on the 8th. Monsr SÉONBLEN MARTIN joined the unit for duty as interpreter on the 10th. Strength of unit on the 13th in FRANCE – Present with unit - officers 30 - other ranks 745 ; Detached for instruction with the 1st Div in the line - officers 5, other ranks 14	R.G.B.
" 14th/15th	An advanced billeting party of 1 officer and 1 NCO (mounted) and also the transport & transport personnel of the unit moved by march route to HAMEL via PICQUIGNY, AILLY-SUR-SOMME, ST. SAUVEUR, ARGOEUVES, AMIENS, LONGUEAU, BLANGY-TRONVILLE, FOUILLOY, HAMLET, & VAIRE. The transport of units were brigaded. These two parties were billeted for the night of 14th/15th at ST SAUVEUR HOUR OF MARCH on 14th from LONGPRÉ 1015 " ARRIVAL " " at ST. SAUVEUR 1700 " MARCH - 15th from " 0900 " ARRIVAL " " at HAMEL 1930	Ref. 125th Bde ORDER No 1 d. 13/3/17 Ref. Mops FRANCE SHEETS {ABBEVILLE 14 / AMIENS 17 Scale 1/100 000
"	The unit, less 2 officers and 20 other ranks, who proceeded for instruction at 4th Army School of Instruction in musketry on the 14th left ERONDELLE on the 15th by march route for LONGPRÉ via LIERCOURT, FONTAINE and VIEULAINE.	Ref 125th BDE ORDER No 2 d.14/3/17 Ref. Map FRANCE SHEET ABBEVILLE 14 Scale 1/100 000

Army Form C. 2118.

1/8th LANCASHIRE FUSILIERS.

WAR DIARY
~~INTELLIGENCE SUMMARY~~
(Erase heading not required.)

Instructions regarding War Diaries and Intelligence Summaries are contained in F.S. Regs., Part II and the Staff Manual respectively. Title pages will be prepared in manuscript.

Hour, Date, Place	Summary of Events and Information	Remarks and references to Appendices
ERONDELLE MARCH 14th/15th	Hour of MARCH from ERONDELLE 0800 " ARRIVAL AT LONGPRÉ 1030 On arrival at LONGPRÉ the unit entrained for CORBIE leaving at 1100, arriving at 1330. From here the unit marched by platoons at 100 yards interval to HAMEL arriving at 1630. Billets having been allotted by the advanced billeting party which had arrived by road from ST SAUVEUR at 1330. Platoons marched straight to their respective billets. The unit was billeted in 1½ hours.	Ref Map FRANCE Sheet AMIENS -17 scale 1/100,000 R.Y.B.
HAMEL 16th	In billets at HAMEL. The men were in barns, average number to a barn - 20. There were still very few cases of sickness in spite of the severe nature of the weather.	R.Y.B.
" 17th	The advanced embarkation party who had been attached to units of the 1st Divⁿ in the trenches rejoined the Batⁿ viz. 2L^t A. DESQUESNES, 2L^t A.B. WARING, 2L^t J. BROADBENT, 2L^t W.B. BROADBENT and 14 other ranks. The fifth officer Lt D. HORNER* had died some days before from sickness.	*(Not yet officially reported) R.Y.B.

Army Form C. 2118.

WAR DIARY

~~INTELLIGENCE SUMMARY.~~

1st/8th LANCASHIRE FUSILIERS.

(Erase heading not required.)

Instructions regarding War Diaries and Intelligence Summaries are contained in F.S. Regs., Part II and the Staff Manual respectively. Title pages will be prepared in manuscript.

Hour, Date, Place	Summary of Events and Information	Remarks and references to Appendices
HAMEL MARCH 18th/21st	CAPT A. CLARKE proceeded for attachment to a unit of the 1st Divn in the trenches on the 18th rejoining the unit on the 20th. Major M.G. BIRD and Capt A.L.B. SHAW proceeded to the trenches for the same purpose on the 20th. Programme of work consisted of instructing the new formations in the attack. Lewis gun instruction and instruction in gas. 2nd Lieut W.D. BROADBENT proceeded to Hospital sick on the 21st.	RWp.
" 22nd	Major M.G. BIRD and Capt A.L.B. SHAW rejoined the unit from attachment to a unit of the 1st Divn in the trenches. The 2 officers and 20 other ranks rejoined the unit from 4th Army School of Instruction at PONT REMY. Strength of unit – officers 39, other ranks 850. Present with unit – officers 34, other ranks 733; Detached in FRANCE officers 5, other ranks 117	RwB.
" 23rd/25th	Hon Lieut Q.M. J. ROBINSON proceeded to ENGLAND on 10 days furlough on the 25th. The unit moved by route march to FEUILLERES on the 25th via CERISY – MERICOURT: FROISSY and ECLUSIER. STARTING POINT. Cross Roads at P.4.D.1.3.	Ref 125th Bde ORDER No 3 d. 24/3/17 Ref Map FRANCE Sheets 62C & 62D scale 1/40 000

WAR DIARY

1st/8th LANCASHIRE FUSILIERS

Army Form C. 2118.

Hour, Date, Place	Summary of Events and Information	Remarks and references to Appendices
HAMEL MARCH 22/25	HOUR OF MARCH 7.0 AM " ARRIVAL 2:30 PM CAPT R.J. MCNICHOL rejoined from hospital on the evening of the 25th	Re-time Ref. 42nd Div R.O. 58 d 23/3/17 (Ref)
FEUILLÈRES 26th/30th	The unit was billeted in dug-outs and cellars amongst the ruins of the village. M. on S. MARTIN transferred to the 1st/5th LANCASHIRE FUS for attachment as interpreter on the 27th The unit was on fatigue duty at BIACHES on the 27th, 28th & 29th	Ref. MAP FRANCE Sheet 62c scale 40000 (N.Y.B.)
" 31st	CAPT A.L.B. SHAW proceeded to MONTIGNY for duty on the staff of the 42nd Div. School of Instruction. - CAPT G. SUTTON proceeded to CAPPY to take over administrative area from the 48th Div. (temporarily) 2Lieut J BROADBENT and 2 O.R. proceeded to BARLEUX for temporary attachment to 429 Fey R.E. 2Lieut D. MCLAINE proceeded to Hospital sick, also 2Lieut H. BUCKLEY.	[Ref Sheet 62 D. B.18.] [Ref Sheet 62 c . G. 36.] [Ref Sheet 62 c N.18]

Army Form C. 2118.

WAR DIARY

INTELLIGENCE SUMMARY.

1st /8th LANCASHIRE FUSILIERS.

(Erase heading not required.)

Instructions regarding War Diaries and Intelligence
Summaries are contained in F.S. Regs., Part II.
and the Staff Manual respectively. Title pages
will be prepared in manuscript.

Hour, Date, Place	Summary of Events and Information	Remarks and references to Appendices
FEUILLERES MARCH 31st	10 days leave to ENGLAND, granted by 3rd Corps, commenced on the 25/3/17 at the average rate of 3 all ranks daily. Numbers who proceed between 25th & 31st :- Officers 1, other ranks 17. Strength of unit on 31st :- Officers 39, other ranks 826; Present with unit :- Officers 28, other ranks 675; Detached :- Officers 11, other ranks 151	Ref 42nd Div Letter No 222/8 d. 15/3/17 Ref. W.F. D'Auvrey D.C. Comg 1/8 Lanc Fus.

125/42

22 N.
8 sheets

Vol 3

"Confidential"

War Diary

of.

1st/8th Lancashire Fusiliers.

To.

1.4.17 — 30.4.17

Volume 24.

Army Form C. 2118.

WAR DIARY
or
INTELLIGENCE SUMMARY
(Erase heading not required)

1st/8th LANCASHIRE FUSILIERS.

Place	Date	Hour	Summary of Events and Information	Remarks and references to Appendices
FEUILLERES	APRIL/17 1st		2nd Lieut L. WATMAN and 2nd Lieut H. FLETCHER rejoined the unit from leave in ENGLAND. 2nd Lieut. H.C. SPEAKMAN and 15 other ranks rejoined the unit from BASE DETAILS EGYPT. The unit was on fatigue duty, repairing the HERBECOURT - BIACHES road.	Ref A.F. FRAINS SHEET 62c 1/40,000 R&B.
"	2nd/5		2nd Lieut H.C. SPEAKMAN relieved 2nd Lieut J. BROADBENT temporally attached to 427 Coy R.E. on the 3rd Capt T.E. THORPE and 2nd Lieut J. BROADBENT proceeded to ENGLAND on 10 days leave on the 4th and 5th respectively. 2nd Lieut. W.B. BROADBENT rejoined from hospital on the 4th. 2nd Lieut C.G. JACOB proceeded to Hospital sick on the 4th. Official record received on the 4th of the death of Lieut D. HORNER. "Died of pneumonia at the 48th C.C.S. in the field 5.3.17"	Ref AF 01810 1/8 Lanc Fus 31/3/17 R&B.
"	5th		The unit moved by march route to PERONNE. HOUR OF MARCH - 4 A.M. " ARRIVAL - 7.15 A.M. On arrival men were allotted their billets and proceeded to work on the PERONNE-DOINGT road.	Ref 125th Bde Order BM.265 d 4/4/17 Ref A.F. Sheet 62c R&B.
PERONNE	6th		Strength of unit :- officers 39, other ranks 834 : present with unit - officers 19, other ranks 554 : detached in FRANCE: officers 20, other ranks 280	R&B.

Army Form C. 2118.

WAR DIARY
INTELLIGENCE SUMMARY. 1st 1/8th LANCASHIRE FUSILIERS
(Erase heading not required.)

Instructions regarding War Diaries and Intelligence Summaries are contained in F.S. Regs., Part II. and the Staff Manual respectively. Title pages will be prepared in manuscript.

Place	Date	Hour	Summary of Events and Information	Remarks and references to Appendices
PERONNE.	April 7th		LIEUT A.B. WARING proceeded on 3 weeks special leave to ENGLAND. Number of other ranks who proceeded on 10 days leave to ENGLAND from 1st to 7th = 19. Hon Lieut & Q.M. J. ROBINSON rejoined from 10 days leave in ENGLAND. Mons S. MARTIN rejoined from 1st/5th LANCASHIRE FUSILIERS.	1. AUTHORITY No 5/B4a Sc 454 dd 5.4.17 2. III Corps A848 dd 3.17 R.of J.
"	8th		Unit working on PERONNE - DOINGT and PERONNE - TINCOURT roads. LIEUT COL C. St L. DAVIS, officer commanding the unit, and 2nd LIEUT W.B. BROADBENT proceeded to hospital sick. MAJOR M. G. BIRD, 2nd in command, assumed command of the unit.	R.of J.
"	9th/10th		The unit moved to LONGAVESNES on the 10th. HOUR OF MARCH - 2.15 P.M. HOUR OF ARRIVAL - 5.0 P.M. Mons S. MARTIN (interpreter) proceeded to 1st Div HQ for duty on the 10th	Ref 125th Bde Dm 335 d. 10/4/17 Ref Inf. G2c, E25. R.of J.
LONGAVESNES	11th/12th		The unit working on LONGAVESNES - VILLERS FAUCON road both days. MAJOR A.L.B. SHAW rejoined unit (10th)from duty with #2 Div School, it having ceased to exist. 2nd LIEUT S.A. SPRINGBETT proceeded to hospital sick from #2nd Div Bombing School. Mons C. GOOD joined unit for duty as interpreter on the 12th. Two companies (A Coy and D Coy) with MAJOR A.L.B. SHAW in command moved forward into support of the 1/6TH LANCASHIRE FUSILIERS on the night of the 12th. Move completed by 9.15 P.M.	By Letter #3 Bde G.S. 11/4/15 By Letter Ref 125th Bde G2c R.of J.

1577 Wt.W10791/1773 500,000 1/15 D. D. & L. A.D.S.S./Forms/C. 2118.

Army Form C. 2118.

WAR DIARY
or
INTELLIGENCE SUMMARY. 1/8TH LANCASHIRE FUSILIERS.

(Erase heading not required.)

Place	Date	Hour	Summary of Events and Information	Remarks and references to Appendices
LONGAVESNES	APRIL 13TH		Relief of 1/5/6TH LANCASHIRE FUSILIERS at SAULCOURT completed. HOUR OF MARCH 4 P.M. " ARRIVAL 5.30 P.M. One company "C" Coy. Capt W.M. Stone in command moved forward into outpost to 1/6TH LANCASHIRE FUSILIERS in the night sector of 125th Bde front of the line. Hour of arrival 8 P.M. They relieved one company of the 1/4/7TH LANCASHIRE FUSILIERS. They were [at once moved forward into the line. They joined the left company of the 16TH LANCASHIRE FUSILIERS. the 1/5TH LANCASHIRE FUSILIERS being on their left.] MAP REF OR POSITION HELD. 62c NE. F.16.81 to F.16.35 1/20000 2ND LIEUT D. McLAINE and 2ND LIEUT H. BUCKLEY rejoined the unit from hospital	Ref Bde O.O. / Appen Ref 125th Bde Order No 5 d.11.4.17 Ref 125th Bde Oper Note No 2 d.14.4.17 Ref.
SAULCOURT	14TH		The unit moved S.W. to CARTIGNY, one company proceeding in advance, arriving BAN and working at CATELET. HOUR OF MARCH of UNIT 1 P.M. " ARRIVAL " 4.45 P.M. The company in the line was relieved by a company of the 1/5TH ROYAL WARWICKSHIRE REGT. at 9 P.M. They returned complete having suffered no casualties, and arrived at CARTIGNY at 4.20 A.M. on the 15TH.	Ref Map 62c Ref 125th Bde Order No 7 d.13.4.17 Ref.

WAR DIARY

~~INTELLIGENCE SUMMARY~~ 1st/8th LANCASHIRE FUSILIERS

Army Form C. 2118.

Place	Date	Hour	Summary of Events and Information	Remarks and references to Appendices
CARTIGNY	APRIL 15TH		The unit working at BUIRE and CATELET repairing roads. 2.Lieut C.G.JACOB rejoined the unit from hospital. Strength of unit:- officers 40, other ranks 842; Present with unit:- officers 24, other ranks 522. Detached: officers 16, other ranks 320. Number of other ranks who proceeded on 10 days leave to ENGLAND 8 officers, other ranks 38.	R.g.g.
	16TH		Capt T.E. THORPE rejoined from ten days leave in ENGLAND	R.g.g.
	17TH		The unit moved W. to FEUILLERES Hour of MARCH - 10.30 AM " ARRIVAL - 4.10 PM Capt F.S. BEDALE (R.A.M.C. Medical Officer) proceeded to hospital sick; Capt C.W. FORT 1st/1st East Lancs F.A. joined unit to take his place.	Ref. 2nd D25 Order No 8 of 15/4/17 Ref 62 c. 1/40,000 R.g.g.
FEUILLERES	18TH/20TH		These three days were given up to training. - 2Lt E.D. MICHAELIS and Major A.L.D. SHAW proceeded on ten days leave to ENGLAND on the 18TH & 20TH respectively. 2nd Lt J. BROADBENT rejoined from ten days leave in ENGLAND on the 19TH. Capt R.J. McNICHOL proceeded to Hospital sick on the 20TH.	R.g.g.

Army Form C. 2118.

WAR DIARY
INTELLIGENCE SUMMARY.
1st/8th Lancashire Fusiliers.

(Erase heading not required.)

Place	Date	Hour	Summary of Events and Information	Remarks and references to Appendices
FEUILLÈRES	APRIL 21st		The unit moved S.E. to the following places:- 2 Coys and Batt H.Q to MONS-EN-CHAUSSÉE, 1 Coy to VILLERS-CARBONNEL and 1 Coy to ESTREÉS-EN-CHAUSSÉE. HOUR OF MARCH - 9 A.M. " ARRIVAL of H.Q - 4.30 P.M. Number of other ranks who proceeded on ten days leave to ENGLAND 15th - 21st = 25. Strength of unit :- officers 40, other ranks 842 : Present with unit :- officers 27, other ranks 518. Detached :- Officers 13, other ranks 324.	Ref 125th Div Adm Nog A 20/4/17 and 125th Div Adm BM 17b & 20/4/17 Ref No. 62c 4000 Ref.
MONS EN CHAUSSÉE	22nd		Unit working on roads. 2Lt S.A. SPRINGBETT rejoined unit from Hospital. 2Lt H.A. ATKINSON 3/6th Lancashire Fusiliers joined unit for duty from ENGLAND	Ref.
"	23rd		Unit working on roads near the three villages in which the Companies were billeted.	
	25th		One officer and 104 other ranks proceeded to 4th Army School of Musketry PONT RÉMY to instruction on the 25th. Capt C.W. SUTTON rejoined the unit from temp duty as administrative commandant CAPPY on 23rd Major G.S. CASTLE 1/4th Gloucestershire Regt joined the unit 25th to take over command from Major N.G. BIRD who resumed duties as 2nd I/C.	2d. ABBEVILLE 14 mgt / 102,000 Ref. 62c. Inst / 40,000 Ref.

WAR DIARY

~~INTELLIGENCE~~ SUMMARY. 1st/8th Lancashire Fusiliers.

Army Form C. 2118.

Place	Date	Hour	Summary of Events and Information	Remarks and references to Appendices
MONS EN CHAUSSÉE.	APRIL 26TH/27TH		The unit was divided up during these two days. The following moves took place:- 26th. 2 Platoons ("A" Coy.) to TOULAUCOURT. Ref. Map 1/40,000 62c - (1) Ref 125th Bde S.I. L 25/4/17 27th. A, B & C Coys (no 2 Coy.) to CERISY " " 1/40,000 62c - (2) Ref 125th Bde I D/N 222.55 " HQ and attached " PERONNE " " 62c - (3) Ref 125th Bde " "A" Coy at VILLERS CARBONEL remained. " " 62c B/N 229 - 26/4/17 2nd Lt. H.M. STURT, who had been Adjutant of 42nd Divl Base Depot since APRIL 1916, rejoined the unit on the 26th. (4) Ref 125th Bde W 2 26/4/7 Ref. Strength of unit :- Officers 43, other ranks 842. Present with unit:- Officers 14, other ranks 80 Detached: Officers 29, other ranks 756. Number of other ranks who proceeded on 10 days leave to ENGLAND 22nd to 28th = 40.	R/D.
PERONNE	28TH			Ref 125th Bde O/O No 10 L 29/4/17
"	29TH	1.30 PM / 2.30 PM	H.Q and attached of the unit moved to DOINGT. HOUR OF MARCH . 1.30 PM " ARRIVAL . 2.30 PM	Ref Map 62c R/D.

Army Form C. 2118.

WAR DIARY
or
INTELLIGENCE SUMMARY. 1/8TH LANCASHIRE FUSILIERS

(Erase heading not required.)

Place	Date	Hour	Summary of Events and Information	Remarks and references to Appendices
DOINGT	April 30TH		Under canvas in DOINGT. Site of camp:- Map 62E.7.36.K.3.7. 2 Platoons at FOUCAUCOURT; A, B, C Coys (ans 2 Coys) at CERISY, and the Coy at VILLERS-CARBONEL all rejoined the unit on the 30TH.	R.J.

G.S. Castle Major
Commanding 1/8th Lancashire Fusiliers.
30/4/17.

Vol. 4

23.N.
8 sheets

CONFIDENTIAL

WAR DIARY
of.
1st/8th LANCASHIRE FUSILIERS

From 1st May 1917   To 31st May 1917

Volumn 25.

Army Form C.2118.

WAR DIARY
INTELLIGENCE SUMMARY.
(Erase heading not required.)

1/8th LANCASHIRE FUSILIERS

Place	Date	Hour	Summary of Events and Information	Remarks and references to Appendices
DOINGT	MAY 1st 1917		Lieut A.B WARING and 2nd Lieut E.B. MICHAELIS returned from 10 days leave in ENGLAND on 31st. Capt. F.S. BEDALE rejoined unit from hospital, and Capt. W. FORT rejoined 1/5/1st EAST LANC Fd Amb. 2/Lieut S.A. SPRINGETT posted to 42nd Div HQ for temporary duty as D.V. Ammun Officer. Capt. C.W. SUTTON and Lieut E. FAIRHURST proceeded on 10 days leave in ENGLAND.	RCB
"	2nd		Unit moved to TINCOURT into billets. Hour of march - 10.30 am. " " Arrival - 12.30 pm.	Ref 125 Bde Bm1904/5/17 Ref Map 62c 29/15
TINCOURT	3rd		The 42nd Division relieved the 48th Division in the Left Sector of III Corps front. Unit moved forward and relieved 1/4th Gloucester Regt in support 1/6 left Battn of 125th Bde front. Battn supported 1/5/6th LANCASHIRE FUSILIERS. Disposition of unit - Batt HQ and 2 Coys (B+D) at St EMILIE in Railway Cutting Rg62c E24a Ref 62 F15. 2 Coys (A+C) at LEMPIRE in Billets. The support line which was the main line of resistance, to be held by the two forward companies in case of attack, consisted of seven strong posts in front of the village. Map ref of the line F.1.b.c 1.b F8.d. The 104 OR at School of Musketry PONT REMY rejoined the unit. Major A.L.B. SHAW rejoined unit from ten days leave in ENGLAND	Ref 125 Bde OO No 11 30/4/17 RCB

1577 Wt.W10791/1773 500,000 1/15 D.D. & L. A.D.S.S./Forms/C. 2118.

WAR DIARY
OR
INTELLIGENCE SUMMARY.   1/6 /8TH LANCASHIRE FUSILIERS

Army Form C. 2118.

(Erase heading not required.)

Instructions regarding War Diaries and Intelligence Summaries are contained in F. S. Regs., Part II. and the Staff Manual respectively. Title pages will be prepared in manuscript.

Place	Date	Hour	Summary of Events and Information	Remarks and references to Appendices
ST EMILIE	4TH	—	In support to Left Batt of 125TH BDE FRONT. Disposition as on the 3RD. Capt R. J. McNichol returned to unit from Hospital. 2ND Lieut H. Buckley proceeded on 10 days leave to England. Strength of Battn: officers 43, other ranks 831. Present with unit:- officers 27, other ranks 468. Detailed:- officers 16, other ranks 363.	R.W.D.
"	5TH		The 125TH BDE was relieved by 126TH BDE. The unit was relieved by 1/5TH EAST LANCS REGT, and moved back into Divl Reserve to the Left BDE of the Divl front. Relief completed by 11 p.m. Disposition of unit: Batt HQ and 2 Coys (A+C) in SAULCOURT area. 2 Coys (B+D) found in EPEHY.	Ref 125TH BDE OO.17.Q13 d 2/5/17. Ref 62c E10b 62c F8a - F1b Ref 62c F8. R.W.D.
SAULCOURT	6TH / 7TH		Disposition as on the 5TH. Unit working at night on defences at MALASISE FARM. Capt F. S. BEDALE proceeded on 10 days leave to ENGLAND on the 7TH.	R.W.D.
	8TH / 9TH		The 125TH BDE relieved the 127TH BDE in Divisional Left Sector. The unit moved forward to relieve the 3/6TH MANCHESTER REGT in the LEFT SUB-SECTOR of the 125TH BDE front. Relief completed by 2.30 a.m. on the 9TH.	Ref 125TH BDE OO.14 d 6/5/17.

WAR DIARY

Army Form C. 2118.

INTELLIGENCE SUMMARY
(Erase heading not required.)

1st/8th LANCASHIRE FUSILIERS.

Instructions regarding War Diaries and Intelligence Summaries are contained in F. S. Regs., Part II. and the Staff Manual respectively. Title pages will be prepared in manuscript.

Place	Date	Hour	Summary of Events and Information	Remarks and references to Appendices
—	May 8th/9th	—	Disposition of unit:- Batt. HQ. 1 Coy. Support Line. 2 Coy Main Line of Resistance - "A" & "B" Coys 1 Coy Outpost Line. - "D" Coy (Capt T.E. Thorpe in command) Map Ref. - 57c X.26.c.48. " - 57c X 27 & 22 & X 21 a 32. " - 57c X 28 b. & b X 21 b 49. " - 57c X 23 c 44 & X 17 d 26. The right Batt of the 8th Divn was on the left and the 1st/7th Lancashire Fusiliers on the right. (Regt)	
In the Line.	9th to 12th		The line was very quiet during the whole of the four days, the enemy shelling mostly in the rear on EPEHY and VILLERS GUISLAIN (Left sear). There was a great deal of activity in the air, but very few enemy machines flew further than our outpost line. An air-fight took place on the 10th between nine British machines and two enemy machines. One of ours was brought down and fell in front of the main line of resistance in the right sub-sector. The only casualty was 1 other rank, killed on the 12th by shell fire, in the main line of resistance. Work was carried on each night strengthening the outpost & main line of resistance.	(Regt)

Army Form C. 2118.

WAR DIARY
INTELLIGENCE SUMMARY. 1st/8th LANCASHIRE FUSILIERS.

(Erase heading not required.)

Instructions regarding War Diaries and Intelligence Summaries are contained in F. S. Regs., Part II. and the Staff Manual respectively. Title pages will be prepared in manuscript.

Place	Date	Hour	Summary of Events and Information	Remarks and references to Appendices
IN THE LINE	May 12th/13th		The unit was relieved by the 1st/5th LANCASHIRE FUSILIERS on the right of the 12th/13th. Relief complete by 1.30 am on the 13th. The unit moved back to PEIZIERE into outpost to left sub sector.	Ref 12.5 - 7th Bde OO 15. 11/5/17
PEIZIERE	13th/16th		Unit in cellars and shelters in PEIZIERE. CAPT G.W. SUTTON and LIEUT E. FAIRHURST rejoined unit working each night on defences of left out sector. LIEUT A. CLYNER and 2nd LIEUT F. BAILEY proceeded on 10 days leave to ENGLAND on the 16th.	RQB
"	16th/17th		The unit relieved the 1st/5th LANCASHIRE FUSILIERS in the left sub-sector of 125th BDE on the 17th. Disposition of unit as before with "D" Coy in Support Line, "B" & "C" Coys in Main Line of Resistance and "A" Coy, CAPT A CLARKE in command, in the outpost line.	Ref 12.5 7th Bde OO 15 11/5/17
IN THE LINE	17th/18th		The two days were very quiet. The weather was bad, Aero observation very poor. A patrol went out to try and locate an enemy machine gun in x 24 a 77 but failed to do so. The unit suffered no casualties.	RQB

1577 Wt.W10791/1773 500,000 1/15 D. D. & L. A.D.S.S./Forms/C. 2118.

Army Form C. 2118.

WAR DIARY
of
INTELLIGENCE SUMMARY. 1st/8th LANCASHIRE FUSILIERS.

(Erase heading not required.)

Instructions regarding War Diaries and Intelligence Summaries are contained in F. S. Regs., Part II. and the Staff Manual respectively. Title pages will be prepared in manuscript.

Place	Date	Hour	Summary of Events and Information	Remarks and references to Appendices
IN THE LINE	17th/18th		Strength of unit on 18th: officers 41, other ranks 780. Present with unit: officers 29, other ranks 561. Detached: officers 12, other ranks 219.	R.S.B.
"	18th/19th		The 42nd Divn was relieved by the 2nd Cavalry Divn. The 125th Bde was relieved by 3rd Cavalry Bde from 1 Regt. The unit was relieved on the night of 18th/19th by the 5th Lancer Regt and one Squadron of 4th Hussar Regt. Relief complete by 1.30 a.m on the 19th. The unit moved back into billets and bivouacs at Villers Faucon.	Ref. 125th Bde 100-16-16/5/17. R.S.B.
VILLERS FAUCON	20th		The 125th Bde moved by march route to 15th Corps area into billets at EQUANCOURT. Hour of March 1 P.m. " Arrival 4 P.m.	Ref. 125th Bde J. 90.17-19/5/17. Ref. No. A. 57/552 2000. R.S.B. R.S.B.
EQUANCOURT	21st/22nd		Unit in billets and shelters in EQUANCOURT. 2nd Lieut H. Buckley rejoined unit from 10 days leave in ENGLAND on the 20th 2nd Lieut E.H. Bryant 3/8th Batt Lanc Fuss joined unit for duty from ENGLAND on the 22nd	R.S.B.

Army Form C. 2118.

WAR DIARY
of
INTELLIGENCE SUMMARY.

1st/8th LANCASHIRE FUSILIERS

(Erase heading not required.)

Instructions regarding War Diaries and Intelligence Summaries are contained in F. S. Regs., Part II. and the Staff Manual respectively. Title pages will be prepared in manuscript.

Place	Date	Hour	Summary of Events and Information	Remarks and references to Appendices
EQUANCOURT	22/9/23		125TH BDE. relieved the 60TH BDE in the line on night 22ND/23RD. The unit relieved the 6TH KING'S SHROPSHIRE LIGHT INFANTRY in the right sector of the Bde FRONT. Relief complete by 1.15 AM 23RD.	Ry 125 Bde O/S 20/9/17 Ry Map 57C SE 1/20,000
IN THE LINE	23RD		The unit's front was held by 3 Coys, one the forefront with one platoon in support) and 1 Coy in reserve. LINE HELD — Map 57C SE 1/20,000. R14 d 50 — R14 b 49 Batt " " " In Sunken Road R20 a 28 — R13 d 91 POSITION OF A HQ and RESERVE COY. — " " " The day was quiet. 2ND LIEUT W. H. STRUTHERS proceeded on ten days leave to ENGLAND.	Reg.
"	24TH		At 3.50 AM. the enemy heavily shelled our front line, centre company. This lasted fifteen minutes but nothing else followed. The centre company had 1 O.R. killed and 2 O.R. wounded. At 5 P.M. the enemy heavily shelled the sunken road for about five minutes. The reserve company suffered one casualty viz 1 O.R. wounded. A good deal of aircraft activity during the day. One of our machines was driven down but landed safely south of GOUZEAUCOURT.	

WAR DIARY
INTELLIGENCE SUMMARY.

1/8th LANCASHIRE FUSILIERS

Army Form C. 2118.

Place	Date	Hour	Summary of Events and Information	Remarks and references to Appendices
IN THE LINE	24th		The centre company sent out a fighting patrol & 1 Officer, 2Lt C.G. JACOB and 10 O.R. with the object of obtaining an identification of the enemy opposite by bringing back a prisoner. They went out at 11.20 p.m. and stayed out for over 2 hours but were unable to locate a small enemy position nor did they meet an enemy patrol.	Ref 125th Bde Y8 24/5/17 PGG.
"	25th/26th		The unit was relieved by 21st Batt MIDDLESEX REGT. on the night of the 25th/26th. Relief complete by 3.20 a.m. on the 26th. During the relief at 1 a.m. the enemy opened a heavy fire on our lines. The last platoon to be relieved was caught up by the barrage when filing out down the communication trench. During this barrage the enemy raided (&) capturing 1 O.R. and a Lewis Gun & the relieving Battalion. We suffered two casualties 1 O.R. killed and 1 O.R. wounded. The unit, on relief, moved into Bde Reserve area in BERTINCOURT.	Ref 125th Bde OO No.19 24/5/17 PGG.
BERTINCOURT	27th/31st		Here the time was given up to training. The 1 O.R. wounded on 26th died in Hospital on the 27th. 2 Lieut C.G. JACOB and 1 O.R. were accidentally wounded during bombing practice on the 29th. Number of other ranks who proceeded on ten days leave to ENGLAND during the month 113. Strength of unit on 31st, officers 42, other ranks 777. Present with unit:- 29 officers, 555 other ranks. Detached 3. officers 13, other ranks 222.	PGG

G.P. Carter Major
Commanding 1/8 Lancashire Fus.

Vol 5

CONFIDENTIAL

WAR DIARY

of

1st/8th LANCASHIRE FUSILIERS

From 1/6/17 to 30/6/17

Volume 26.

WAR DIARY

INTELLIGENCE SUMMARY

1/8th LANCASHIRE FUSILIERS.

Army Form C. 2118.

Place	Date	Hour	Summary of Events and Information	Remarks and references to Appendices
BERTINCOURT	JUNE/1917. 1st		MAJOR G.E. HOPE M.C., GRENADIER GUARDS, joined the unit to take over command.	Ref map FRANCE 57c.
			MAJOR G.S. CASTLE M.C., 1/4th GLOUCESTERSHIRE REGT, who proceeded to join 1/5th LANCASHIRE FUSs for duty as 2nd in command.	Ref.B
"	2nd/4th		Time given up to training. — On 3rd:- LIEUT A. CLYMER and 2nd LT F. BAILEY returned from 7 and 10 days leave in ENGLAND. 2nd LIEUT H.C. SPEAKMAN and 2nd LIEUT S.J. WHITE & G.V.H. PROCTER proceeded on attachment to 427 FLD COY RE and were replaced by 25 other ranks rejoined unit from other ranks with 2nd LIEUT M.A. STURT in command. The same number of other ranks. CAPT A. CLARKE proceeded to hospital sick.	Ref.B
IN THE LINE	5th/6th		The 125th BDE relieved the 126th BDE in the right sector of 42nd Divl front, in the left sector of III Corps front. The unit relieved the 1st/5th EAST LANCASHIRE REGt in the left sector of the BDE front. Relief complete by 12.55 AM on 6th. Disposition of units:-	Ref 125 BDE D.O. No 20 3/6/17
			BATT HQ. - Ref 57c Q8b 2/4. HAVRINCOURT WOOD { B Coy in Reserve Coy.4Qd." " Q8 d 8/8. D " " Support. " " Q4 c 0/9 - Q3 c 2/7. (A + C Coys " Front Line - " Q4 a 6/1 - Q3 a 5/1.	Ref.B
			The above disposition was changed later, the front line being sub. divided into 3 Coy fronts, each finding its own support.	Ref.B

WAR DIARY

INTELLIGENCE SUMMARY

Army Form C. 2118.

1/8TH LANCASHIRE FUSILIERS.

Place	Date	Hour	Summary of Events and Information	Remarks and references to Appendices
IN THE LINE	JUNE 7TH/8TH		During the day no work was able to be carried out. During the night unit, working with the 1/6TH LANC FUS who came up each night to assist in the work, from LEFT RESERVE baps (D&E) running 300 yds out from the firing line. These two sap heads were being joined up to make new firing line. Two officers were wounded during the night 6,7/8TH viz 2ND LIEUTS R. SHARPE and E.V. HARRISON and proceeded to hospital.	Ref Map FRANCE 57C 20,000 to 57C S2 10,000 Ryy.
"	9TH/14TH		Work carried out each night. New trenches dug from "D" to "E" sap and trench running from "E" sap to join up with unit on left. Wire was put up in front of all new trenches dug. The enemy tried to hinder the work by oversing machine gun fire and trench mortars from advanced positions in front of the "HINDENBURG" LINE. On 9TH - 2ND LIEUT W.H. STRUTHERS rejoined unit from 10 days leave in ENGLAND. On 10TH - LIEUT R.G. BIRD proceeded on " " " " On 10TH - CAPT W.E. LECOINDER rejoined unit for duty from ENGLAND (having left unit sick Sept/1915) On 14TH - 2ND LIEUT L.H. PETTIT was admitted to hospital suffering from "chill plask" (wounded)	Ryy.
"	15TH/16TH		Unit was relieved in the line by 1ST/7TH LANCASHIRE FUSILIERS. Relief completed by 1.50 AM on 16TH Unit came out into BDE RESERVE in HAVRINCOURT WOOD	Ref 1/5 BDE 0022 CONT'D

WAR DIARY
or
INTELLIGENCE SUMMARY. 1st /8th LANCASHIRE FUSILIERS.

Army Form C. 2118.

Place	Date	Hour	Summary of Events and Information	Remarks and references to Appendices
IN THE LINE (CONTINUED)	15TH/16TH		Disposition of unit after relief:- "B" & "D" Coys (in intermediate line) 37c - Q8 a.c. 29.40 " " " : Q8 d.2.f. Batt HQ and 'A' 'C' Coys " : Q8 d.2.f. Total casualties during tour in front line:- Killed - 10 other ranks: Wounded - 3 officers, 18 other ranks: Gassed - 3 other ranks. Strength of unit:- officers, 39; other ranks 740: Present with unit:- officers 27; other ranks 565.	Ref Map France 57c 1/40,000 & 57c 1/10,000 (RB)
HAVRINCOURT WOOD	17TH/20TH		Unit sent working parties up each night to assist units in the line. On 17th 2nd Lieut H.C. SPEAKMAN proceeded to RUYAULCOURT for Lty as Town Major On 20th 2nd Lieuts. J WHITE and G.V.H. PROCTER rejoined unit from 10 days leave in ENGLAND	Ry57: (RB)
"	21ST/22ND		On night 21st/22nd, 126TH BDE relieved the 125TH BDE in the line. The unit remained in BDE RESERVE. Disposition of unit as before except for one company "D" Coy which was in the "second line". Coy HQ at J.P18.d.4/4. The unit worked on intermediate and second lines and carried out training when possible.	Ref 125TH BDE OO 23 19/6/17 (CONTINUED)

Army Form C. 2118.

WAR DIARY
INTELLIGENCE SUMMARY

1st/8th LANCASHIRE FUSILIERS.

(Erase heading not required.)

Place	Date	Hour	Summary of Events and Information	Remarks and references to Appendices
HAVRINCOURT WOOD (CONTINUED)	27th / 28th		On 23rd Capt R.J. McNicol proceeded on 3 weeks leave in ENGLAND. On 24th Capt T.E. THORPE M.C. proceeded to join staff of III Corps School of Instruction for duty as an instructor. On 26th Lieut R.G. BIRD adjoined unit from 10 days leave in ENGLAND. On 27th 2nd Lieut S.A. SPRINGBETT proceeded on 10 days leave in ENGLAND. On 28th Lt Col O.St L DAVIES adjoined unit from ENGLAND (sick)	Ref map France 57c 1/40,000 Ref 125 Bde Order 28/6/17 Reg.
"	29th		The unit was relieved by 1/5th Lancashire Fusiliers and moved back into rest billets in YTRES. Move completed by 4 AM on 30th.	
YTRES	30th		Lt Col O.St L DAVIES Re-assumed command of the unit. Major G.E. HOPE M.C. remaining as 2nd in command. Strength of unit :- officers 37; other ranks 703: Present with unit :- officers 26; other ranks 533: Detached :- officers 11; other ranks 170.	

Major
Commanding 1/8 Lanc. Fus.

125/42

Y56

25 N.
3 sheets

CONFIDENTIAL

WAR DIARY

1st/8th LANCASHIRE FUSILIERS

From 1/7/17

T. 31/7/17

Volume 27.

Army Form C. 2118.

WAR DIARY

~~INTELLIGENCE SUMMARY~~ of 1st/8th Lancashire Fusiliers.

(Erase heading not required.)

Instructions regarding War Diaries and Intelligence Summaries are contained in F.S. Regs., Part II. and the Staff Manual respectively. Title pages will be prepared in manuscript.

Place	Date	Hour	Summary of Events and Information	Remarks and references to Appendices
YTRES.	July 1st/4th		Unit in rest - Billets in YTRES. Time given up to training.	Ref France 57^c R.g.9.
			On 2nd Lieut A. Clynes proceeded to join 125 Machine Gun Coy to take up duties of transport officer. On 4th 2nd Lieut C. G. JACOB rejoined unit from hospital.	
"	5th.		The unit was inspected by the 125th Infy Bde Comdr, Brig Gen H. FARGUS C.M.G. D.S.O. who had taken over command from Brig Gen H. C. FRITH C.B. on 23 June/17.	R.g.9.
"	6th.		The 58th Divn relieved the 42nd Divn. The Divn on relief moved north to an area about BAPAUME into 3rd Army Reserve.	Ry/42d 57^c & W.D 300. Ry/125 Bde WA23 10/7/17. Ry/125 Bde 100.26 5/7/17.
			The 125th Infy Bde moved by route march to GONIECOURT. Starting Point Cross Roads. Bus 014 8 2/0. Hour of Start 6.0 A.M. Hour of Arrival 11.30 A.M.	
			The unit was in camp outside the village. Colt. O.St.L. Davies proceeded to the Base as medically unfit. Major G. E. HOPE M.C. assumed command again.	R.g.9.
GONIECOURT.	7th/8th.		Strength of unit on 7th :- Officers 39; other ranks 700; Present with unit :- Officers 28; other ranks 553; Detached :- officers 11; other ranks 147.	R.g.9

WAR DIARY

INTELLIGENCE SUMMARY.

1/8th LANCASHIRE FUSILIERS.

Army Form C. 2118.

Place	Date	Hour	Summary of Events and Information	Remarks and references to Appendices
GOMMECOURT	July 9th/15th		The weeks training consisted of bombing, musketry, bayonet fighting, drill and route-marching. On 10th - 2nd Lieut H.C. SPEAKMAN rejoined unit for duty from ROUALCOURT where he had been acting as Town Major. - 2nd Lieut H.M. STURT and 25 O.R. rejoined unit from attachment to 427 Coy R.E. - 2nd Lieut C.G. JACOB proceeded to ENGLAND on 10 days leave. On 12th - 2nd Lieut S.A. SPRINGBETT rejoined unit from 10 days leave in ENGLAND. On 15th - Capt W.M. STONE proceeded to ENGLAND on 14 days leave.	RSB.
"	16th/22nd		This weeks training was similar to the week before but more advanced training in attack practice and rifle-devotions was carried out. On 21st - 2nd Lieut D. McLAINE proceeding to ENGLAND on 10 days leave. Strength of unit on 22nd Officers 39; other ranks 664. Present with unit Officers 29; other ranks 557; Detached; Officers 10; other ranks 113.	RSB.
"	23rd/31st		Training carried on - On 23rd - 2nd Lieut. C.G. JACOB rejoined unit from 10 days leave in ENGLAND. On 26th - Major N.G. BIRD proceeded on 10 days leave in ENGLAND. " 28th - 2/Lt H.D. IVERS " " " " " 4th Lieut F.B. TURNER " to Hospital Sick " 29th - 2nd Lt F.H. BRYANT " " " "	RSB.

CONFIDENTIAL.

WAR DIARY

of

1/8th Lancashire Fusiliers

From 1st August 1917 — To 31st August 1917

Volume 98

Army Form C. 2118.

WAR DIARY
or
INTELLIGENCE SUMMARY.
(Erase heading not required.)

1st / 8th LANCASHIRE FUSILIERS

Place	Date	Hour	Summary of Events and Information	Remarks and references to Appendices
BOMIÉCOURT	AUGT 1st /17		Training continued. Capt. W.M. STONE rejoined unit from 10 days leave in ENGLAND on 31/7/17. 2nd Lt. J. BROADBENT evacuated to No.1 Sanitary Convt. Station for V.D.H. illness on or about 31/7/17. 2nd Lt. D. McLAINE rejoined unit from 10 days leave in ENGLAND on 2nd. Lieut. F/S TURNER rejoined unit from hospital (sick) on the 2nd. 2/Lt. W.S. BROADBENT evacuated to hospital sick on the 2nd. Capt. W.M. STONE evacuated to hospital accidentally wounded on the 6th.	R.S.B.
"	8/8/17		Training continued. Major M.G. BIRD rejoined unit from 10 days leave in ENGLAND on 8th. 2nd Lt. H. BYERS " " " " " 9th. Capt. W.M. STONE " on the 10th. Lieut. F/S TURNER proceeded to hospital (sick) on 10th. 2nd Lt. H. THRUSH proceeded on 10 days leave in ENGLAND on the 13th. The following reinforcements joined the unit on 29th 66 other ranks on 30th 66 O.R. 2nd Lt. W.H. TAYLOR from 6th Reserve Battn. to take over duties. 2nd Lt. W.H. TAYLOR from 6th Reserve Bn. " " " 50 other ranks " 11th, 62 other ranks " " " Strength of unit now 10 officers, 38 other ranks, 884. Strength now 24 officers, 419 other ranks. 10 ticketed 14 officers 1653 other ranks.	R.S.B.

(Sgd) Lt. Col. B. Shaw, K4,0.
for O.C. 1/8th Lanc. Fusiliers.

Army Form C. 2118.

WAR DIARY
or
INTELLIGENCE SUMMARY.
(Erase heading not required.)

1/8 LANCASHIRE FUSILIERS

Place	Date	Hour	Summary of Events and Information	Remarks and references to Appendices
BONIECOURT	15TH 1917		Journey continued. Capt. A Desquesnes and 2nd Lt. D.G. Bird proceeded on 10 days leave in England on the 15th St. 2nd Lt. H.L. Simpson and 2nd Lt. P.W. Ladmore joined unit for duty from 8 Batt. Lanc. Fus. England.	R.Y.B
BONIECOURT	20TH		Unit joined by rail and moved to Boozincourt N.W. of Albert. Hour of March 9.30 a.m. Arrival 1.15 p.m.	Ref 1st app 1916/17 Ref 2nd app 1917 5000 R.8.3 2000
BOOZINCOURT	21st 22nd 23rd		The unit entrained for the north at Albert at 1.21 a.m. on the 23rd and arrived at Godewaerswelde near Poperinghe at 12.15 p.m. the same day. Ref. Map. France N° 27 Belgium N° 27	Ref 1st app 23rd A1 N° 10 23/8/17
BELGIUM 27 FRANCE 27 L6 G.S.4	24/8/17 27		On arrival unit moved to a training camp in L.14.b. Journey carried on. On 26th 2nd Lt. H. Thrush rejoined from 10 days leave in England. 25th 2nd Lt. H.M. Sturt and 25 O.R. proceeded to join 427 Field by R.E. as permanent working party. On 27th Capt. A Desquesnes and 2nd Lt. D.G. Bird rejoined from 10 days leave in England. 26th Capt. A.B. Waring who had transferred to join a unit of 15 AD in the line on the 25th for temporary duty rejoined A Coy. (Sgd) A. L.L.B. Shaw Major for O.C. 1/8 Lanc. Fusiliers	R.G.B. R.S.B.

Army Form C. 2118.

WAR DIARY
or
INTELLIGENCE SUMMARY. 1/8th LANCASHIRE FUSILIERS
(Erase heading not required).

Instructions regarding War Diaries and Intelligence Summaries are contained in F. S. Regs., Part II. and the Staff Manual respectively. Title pages will be prepared in manuscript.

Place	Date	Hour	Summary of Events and Information	Remarks and references to Appendices
BELGIUM 28 N.W.	AUG 28		Training continued	J.W.
H.11	29		Unit moved into the Forward Area, by rail and road to POPERINGHE and by road to the neighbourhood of GOLDFINCH CHATEAU where it bivouaced.	J.W.
15.9.b.7	30		We got here 287 Officers and O.R. who moved blind no ditch at the conjunct and were moved up to NI44 Cot in relief to the 1/5th Lanc Fus. who were in the Front Line	J.W.
	31		Still in support	J.W.

(sgd) A.H.B. Shaw Major
fr O/C 1/8th Lanc Fusiliers

Vol 8

125/2

27.N.
6 sheets

CONFIDENTIAL

WAR DIARY.

of

1/8TH. LANCASHIRE FUSILIERS.

From 1-9-17. TO 30-9-17.

VOL. 29.

Army Form C. 2118.

WAR DIARY

INTELLIGENCE SUMMARY

(Erase heading not required.)

1/8 LANCASHIRE FUSILIERS.

Place	Date	Hour	Summary of Events and Information	Remarks and references to Appendices
BELGIUM 28 N.W. SQ. FARM. C.30 b.7.8.	SEPT. 1917. 1ST		On the night of the 1st/2nd the BATTALION took over the FRONT LINE, relieving the 1/6 LAN. FUS. Distribution :- Two Coys. in FRONT LINE and two in RESERVE. Batt. H.Q. were at SQUARE FARM in the LEFT SUB-SECTOR, the RIGHT SUB-SECTOR being occupied by the 1/5 and 1/7 LAN. FUS.	REF. 125 BGDE. O.O. No 33. Q.7.
	2ND		Situation unchanged Casualties light.	Q.7.
	3RD		Due to the activity of our ARTILLERY in the neighbourhood of BORRY FARM, BECK HOUSE and IBERIAN on the morning of the 3rd, part of the garrison of the FRONT LINE was withdrawn to close support at "STAND To". Original positions were occupied again at dusk. Capt. A. DESQUESNES Commanding "D" Coy. admitted to HOSP. wounded on this date.	REF. 125 BGDE. Y.4. H.Q.
	4TH		ARTILLERY programme similar to yesterday. Part of the garrison of the FRONT LINE withdrawn till dusk. On the night of the 4th/5th the UNIT less "D" COY, which remained in the LINE, was relieved by one Coy. of 1/6 LAN. FUS. and two Coys. of 1/6 MANCHESTERS. THE COMPANIES relieved went back to positions previously occupied when in SUPPORT	REF. 125 BGDE. O.O. No. 34. Q.7.
	5TH		Situation unchanged.	Q.7.

WAR DIARY

INTELLIGENCE SUMMARY

1/8 LANCASHIRE FUSILIERS.

Army Form C. 2118.

(Erase heading not required.)

Place	Date	Hour	Summary of Events and Information	Remarks and references to Appendices
	AUG. 1917. 6th	(? Sept.)	BORRY FARM attacked by 1/5 LAN. FUS. and BECK HOUSE and IBERIAN by 1/6 LAN. FUS. ZERO 7.30 a.m. D COY. 1/8 LAN. FUS. was in support to 1/6 LAN. FUS. but was not called upon to render assistance. Wiring and carrying parties were also detailed by 1/8 LAN. FUS. for Objectives mentioned above. 2nd LIEUT. G.H.V. PROCTER + LIEUT BAILEY killed, and 2nd LIEUT. H. SIMPSON wounded, were among the casualties of this date. The above Objectives were lost after several enemy counter-attacks.	REF. 125 BDE. O.O. 35. J.T.
	7th		The Unit was relieved by the 6th MANCHESTER REGT. and on relief proceeded to TORONTO CAMP. Total casualties during period in the LINE - 4 OFFICERS. 110 O.R.	REF. 125 BDE O.O. 36. J.T.
TORONTO CAMP. G18 a 4.7	8th/13th		Rest and general Training. Effective strength of Unit on 8th - 22 Officers. 666 O.R. Detached - 11 OFFICERS. 190 O.R. 2.LT. H. BUCKLEY Proceeded to D.H.Q as TRAFFIC CONTROL OFFICER. on 13th	J.T.

Army Form C. 2118.

WAR DIARY

INTELLIGENCE SUMMARY. 1/8th LANCASHIRE FUSILIERS.

(Erase heading not required.)

Instructions regarding War Diaries and Intelligence Summaries are contained in F. S. Regs. Part II. and the Staff Manual respectively. Title pages will be prepared in manuscript.

Place	Date	Hour	Summary of Events and Information	Remarks and references to Appendices
SQUARE FARM.	(Aug. 1917.) 14th	? (b.l)	On the night of the 14th/15th the Battalion relieved 1/8th Manchesters in the FRONT LINE. Distribution:– Two Coys. in LINE and two in RESERVE. Batt. H.Q. at SQUARE FARM. Lt. R. Alderson M.C. rejoined Unit from Div. Traffic Control.	REF. 125 BDE O.O. 37. J.J.
	15th		Post established in front of BECK HOUSE (D19c 96 08) by Patrol which went from 'C' Coy. on the night of 15th with Lt. Alderson M.C. in command.	J.J.
	16th		Still in the LINE. Situation unchanged. Lt. W.H. Struthers rejoined from Divl Base Depot Batt.	J.J.
	17th		Unit relieved by 4th South African Regt. on the night of 17th/18th and on relief proceeded by rail from Asylum Ypres to Ayr Camp. Total Casualties in LINE – 15 O.R. Capt. W.E. Lecomber to Hosp. Sick.	REF. 125 BDE O.O. 38. J.J.

WAR DIARY
or
~~INTELLIGENCE SUMMARY~~

1/8TH. LANCASHIRE FUSILIERS.

Army Form C. 2118.

Place	Date	Hour	Summary of Events and Information	Remarks and references to Appendices
AYR CAMP. G10d 9.3. L.3 CENTRAL	Aug. 1917. 18th.	? (Left)	Time devoted to rest, making up deficiencies etc. 2nd Lt. STURT rejoined from 427 Field Coy. R.E.	J.P.
JEAN-TER-BIEZEND	19th.		The BATT. moved to SCHOOL CAMP JEAN-TER-BIEZEND by Route March. Hour of march 10-30 a.m.	REF. 125 BDE. O.O.39. J.P.
"	20th/21st		Training consisting chiefly of Close Order Drill was carried out daily during stay at SCHOOL CAMP. A certain amount of time was devoted to bathing, Russian Baths being available in the Area. LT. H. FLETCHER proceeded on 10 days leave to U.K. on 21st.	J.P.
LEDRINGHEM	22nd		The BATT. moved to LEDRINGHEM in the ARNEKE Area, marching to the entraining point at HOPOUTRE (L17.d.6.3). Hour of march 3 p.m. Hour of arrival at ARNEKE 1 a.m. on 23rd.	REF. 125 BDE. O.O. 40. J.P.
"	23rd		Rest.	J.P.

Army Form C. 2118.

WAR DIARY
INTELLIGENCE SUMMARY.
(Erase heading not required.)

1/8TH. LANCASHIRE FUSILIERS.

Instructions regarding War Diaries and Intelligence Summaries are contained in F. S. Regs., Part II. and the Staff Manual respectively. Title pages will be prepared in manuscript.

Place	Date	Hour	Summary of Events and Information	Remarks and references to Appendices
GHYVELDE SHEET 19 40,000	AUG. 1917. 24TH	(? S/Feb)	BATT. moved to GHYVELDE, marching to the entraining point at ESQUELBECQ STATION. Hour of march 5 a.m. Time of arrival at GHYVELDE 11-30 a.m. Accomodation was provided in tents, huts, & billets.	REF. 125 BDE. O.O. No 41. 9/7.
ST IDESBALD	25TH		BATT. moved to ST. IDESBALD taking part in BDE. ROUTEMARCH. Hour of march 1-2 p.m. Hour of arrival 3-45 p.m. Camp accomodation was taken over from 2/7TH. MANCHESTERS. 66TH DIV.	REF. 125 BDE. O.O. No 42. 9/7.
"	26TH / 30TH		Since arrival at ST. IDESBALD the time has been spent chiefly in Training, Bathing, & Reorganizing. Following officers joined the UNIT, from ENGLAND on 27TH :- 2ND LT. G.G. WEBB. 2ND LT. W.S. ASTLEY, 2ND LT. A.W. POTTER.	9/7

George Hell
1/8 LF

Vol 9

CONFIDENTIAL

WAR DIARY

of

1ST/8TH LANCASHIRE FUSILIERS.

From 1/10/17   To 31/10/17

VOLUME 30.

WAR DIARY

Army Form C. 2118.

Instructions regarding War Diaries and Intelligence Summaries are contained in F. S. Regs., Part II. and the Staff Manual respectively. Title pages will be prepared in manuscript.

INTELLIGENCE SUMMARY. 1/8TH Lancashire Fusiliers.
(Erase heading not required.)

Place	Date	Hour	Summary of Events and Information	Remarks and references to Appendices
ST IDESBALD	OCT/17 1ST/4TH		In Camp. Training continued. 2nd Lt T Broadbent rejoined unit from duty at the Base on the 1st. Lieut H T Fletcher rejoined unit from 10 days leave in UK on the 3rd.	Ref Sheet A 1/10/17 DUNKIRK Reg
IN THE LINE	5TH/8TH		On the night of the 5th/6th the unit relieved the 17th Batt. H.L.I. in reserve to the left sub section of the Brigade Front. The unit was in positions along the WEST bank of the YSER in front of NIEUPORT. Batt HQ. at M 27 to 90/65. The unit- supplied the garrison of one platoon for the "PRESQU'ILE". Strength of unit (5th) Officers 24, other ranks 620 - Detached Off. 9 - other ranks 148. Situation was quiet during the period in reserve.	Ref 125 Bde. G.O.43 4/10/17 Ref Sheet S Ref
"	9TH/10TH		On night of 9th/10th 1st Batt Reliefs were carried out, the unit relieving the 1/9th Lanc Fus in the front line in left sub sector. Disposition of unit:- B Coy (left) - D Coy (right) in the Front Line running from M.22 a 3/3 - M.22 c 25/75 - M.28 20/50 A Coy - Left support in the HUITRIES in M.28 a C " - " Right " " - REDAN - M.28 L BATT HQ in "RUBBER HOUSE" M.28 L 80/85 2nd Lt A. Standing and 2nd Lt J H Rick joined unit for duty from ENGLAND on the 10th.	Ref 125 Bde G.O.44 8/10/17 Ref
"	11TH/13TH		Situation generally quiet. Lt Col G. E. Hope (commanding) was missing believed prisoner on the 11th. Major Ali B Shaw 2nd i/c took command	Ref

A3834 Wt.W4973/M687 750,000 8/16 D.D.&L.Ltd. Forms/C.2118/13

WAR DIARY
or
INTELLIGENCE SUMMARY. 1/8TH LANCASHIRE FUSILIERS

Army Form C. 2118.

(Erase heading not required.)

Place	Date	Hour	Summary of Events and Information	Remarks and references to Appendices
IN THE LINE	Oct 7 13TH/16TH		Unit relieved on night 13TH/14TH by 6TH LANC FUS & 1/57 went back into RESERVE. Dispositions as before.	Ref 125 BDE D/N 183 13/10/17 Ref.
"	17TH/21ST		Unit again relieved 1/6TH LANC FUS in the front line. A Coy. C Coy in front line. B Coy. D Coy in support. Situation quiet except for heavy shelling of the REDAN & the bridges over the YSER. Operations – 5 patrols were sent out during the time but gained no contact with the enemy. LIEUT L. WATMAN wounded on 10 days leave to ENGLAND on 18TH.	Ref.
"	21ST/22ND		The 127 INF BDE relieved 125 INF BDE. The unit was relieved by 1/8TH MANCHESTER REGT. On relief unit marched back to RESERVE BDE area. into AUSTRALIA CAMP west of COXYDE.	Ref 125 BDE O45 14/10/17 Ref.
COXYDE	23RD/29TH		Whilst in reserve unit found large working parties by day & night. LT. COL. O. ST. L. DAVIES (former commanding officer) rejoined & took over command again on the 23RD. The following officers joined the unit for duty from ENGLAND. On 23RD 2ND LTS. J.C.J. TOOMER, A.G. GIBBONS, E.G. SPEAKMAN, J.J. MASON " 24TH 2ND LT J.W. WILKINSON " 27TH 2ND LT E.M. ROSE MAJOR A.H.B. SHAW proceeded on 10 days leave to ENGLAND on 27TH	Ref.

Army Form C. 2118.

WAR DIARY
of
INTELLIGENCE SUMMARY. 1st /8th LANCASHIRE FUSILIERS

(Erase heading not required.)

Instructions regarding War Diaries and Intelligence Summaries are contained in F.S. Regs., Part II. and the Staff Manual respectively. Title pages will be prepared in manuscript.

Place	Date	Hour	Summary of Events and Information	Remarks and references to Appendices
LA PANNE	29th/31st		Unit moved into Bde Res Regt Billets in LA PANNE. The 1st/8th Lanc Fus taking over the working parties for the forward area. Training carried out whilst in rest. Strength of unit:- officers 24 other ranks 591 ; Detached officers 18 other ranks 195.	Re 125 Bde 3 Yrs Schd. R/M.

M. Davies Lt Col
Comd 1/8 Lanc Fus.

Vol 10

29 N.
5 sheets
Encl

CONFIDENTIAL.

WAR DIARY
of
1/1st/8th. LANCASHIRE FUSILIERS.

From 1/11/17. to 30/11/17.

Vol. 31.

Army Form C. 2118.

WAR DIARY
INTELLIGENCE SUMMARY
(Erase heading not required.)

1st/8th Lancashire Fusiliers.

Place	Date	Hour	Summary of Events and Information	Remarks and references to Appendices
LA PANNE	NOVEMBER/17 1st/4th		In rest billets in LA PANNE – training continued. Strength of unit:– officers 23 other ranks 587. Detailed officers 19 other ranks 168.	R.S.
"	5th/6th		The 125 Inf Bde relieved the 127 Inf Bde on night 5th/6 & 6th/9th. The unit relieved the 1/8 Manchester Regt on night of 5th/6th in reserve in NIEUPORT. Dispositions as in last tour in the line in October/17. 2nd Lt L. WATMAN rejoined the unit from leave in ENGLAND on the 6th	Ry Maj Shutt's HQ 000 Ry 125 Bde OO 47 5/11/17
IN THE LINE BATT HQ at M.27 b.70/65	7th/9th		In Reserve line – general situation quiet.	R.S.
"	10th/		The unit relieved the 15/6th Lancashire Fusiliers in the front left sub-sector on night of 10th/11th Disposition of unit as in tour 10th/13th Oct/17. Batt HQ in RUBBER MOUSE at M.28 c.80/85. Hon Lieut & QM J. ROBINSON on one month's special leave to ENGLAND	Ry 125 Bde OO 48 8/11/17 M07
"	11th/13th		In Front Line Capt. R.G. BIRD proceeded on one month's special leave to ENGLAND	Ing.

Army Form C. 2118.

WAR DIARY
INTELLIGENCE SUMMARY. 1st /8th. LANCASHIRE FUSILIERS.
(Erase heading not required.)

Place	Date	Hour	Summary of Events and Information	Remarks and references to Appendices
BATT. HQ M 27 b 70/65	NOVEMBER 1917. 14th		The Unit was relieved by 1/6th LANCS. FUSILIERS and on relief proceeded to RESERVE LINES as ordered on 7th inst. Relief took place on night of 14/15th.	REF. 125 BDE. O.O. 49. JWJ.
"	15th / 16th		In RESERVE LINES.	
"	17th		The 125th INF. BDE was relieved by 2 BATTS. 321st FRENCH INF. REGT. and 1 BATT. 116th CHASSEURS on nights of 17/18th, 18/19th, 19/20th. On night of 17/18th the UNIT was relieved by 6th BATT. 321st FRENCH INF. REGT. and on relief proceeded to CANADA CAMP. COXIDE.	REF. 125 BDE O.O. 50. JWJ. JWJ.
CANADA CAMP.	18th		REST.	
"	19th		Unit moved to TETEGHEM. This was the first stage of the march to 1st ARMY AREA. Hour of march from CANADA CAMP - 7.15 a.m. Arrival at ADINKERKE - 9.30 a.m. Unit entrained at ADINKERKE at 10 a.m and arrived at TETEGHEM, after short Route march from Detraining point, at 3 p.m. Lt. R. ALDERSON proceeded on 14 days leave to U.K.	REF. 125 BDE O.O. 51 SHEETS 11, 19 40,000 JWJ.
ESQUELBECQ	20th		Unit marched to ESQUELBECQ and remained in billets there for one night. Hour of March - 9 a.m.	REF. 125. BDE. O.O.52. JWJ.

A5634 Wt.W4973/M687. 750,000 8/16 D.D. & L.Ltd. Forms/C.J113/13.

Army Form C. 2118.

WAR DIARY
of
INTELLIGENCE SUMMARY. 1/8TH LANCASHIRE FUSILIERS
(Erase heading not required.)

Instructions regarding War Diaries and Intelligence Summaries are contained in F. S. Regs., Part II. and the Staff Manual respectively. Title pages will be prepared in manuscript.

Place	Date	Hour	Summary of Events and Information	Remarks and references to Appendices
	NOVEMBER 1917.			
ZERMEZEELE.	21ST.		The Unit moved by Route March to ZERMEZEELE and remained in billets for one night. Hour of March – 10 a.m.	REF. 125 BDE O.O. 53. MAP REF. 1/100,000 SHEET 5A. 1/40,000 " 27. W.P.
WALLON CAPPEL AREA	22nd.		The Unit moved by Route March to STAPLE and WALLON CAPPEL Area where it remained in billets for one night. Hour of March – 9 a.m.	REF. 125 BDE. O.O. 55. Map REFS. as above. W.P.
BOESEGHEM.	23rd/26th		The Unit moved by Route March to BOESEGHEM where it went into billets. Hour of March – 9.10 a.m. The Unit carried out Recreational Training from 23rd to 26th inst. LIEUT H.A. BRAENDLE joined the Unit for duty from ENGLAND on 23rd inst. 2/LIEUT H.M. STURT proceeded on 14 days leave to ENGLAND.	REF. 125 BDE O.O. 56. 1/40,000 SHEETS 27 & 36A. W.P.
GORRE and QUESNOY.	27TH.		The Unit moved by Route March to GORRE and QUESNOY in the BETHUNE Area. Hour of March – 8 a.m. The Unit was billeted in these Villages.	REF. 125 BDE O.O. 58. REF. MAP. 1/40,000 BETHUNE 36A. W.P.

Army Form C. 2118.

WAR DIARY
or
INTELLIGENCE SUMMARY. 1st /8th LANCASHIRE FUSILIERS.
(Erase heading not required.)

Place	Date	Hour	Summary of Events and Information	Remarks and references to Appendices
	NOVEMBER 1917			REF. 125 B.O.E. 0.0.59. RE MAPS 1/40,000 BETHUNE
IN THE LINE	28th		The Unit relieved the 2nd Batt. SOUTH LANCASHIRE REGT. in the LEFT SECTOR of the Brigade Front. Disposition:- B, C & D Coys. in the Front Line. "A" Coy. in Support. Batt. H.Q. at —	
"	29th/30th		In the Line. Situation very quiet. Strength of Unit on 30th:- 27 Officers 551 with Unit. 13 " 132 Detached.	W.P.

WR Daniel Lt. Col.
Cmdg. 1/8th Bn. Lancashire Fusiliers Regt.

30.11.17

Vol II

30 N.
3 sheets

CONFIDENTIAL

War Diary

of

1st 1/8th Lancashire Fusiliers

From 1/11/17 to 31/12/17

Volume 32.

WAR DIARY
of 1st/8th LANCASHIRE FUSILIERS
INTELLIGENCE SUMMARY

Army Form C. 2118.

Place	Date	Hour	Summary of Events and Information	Remarks and references to Appendices
IN THE LINE	December 1st / 3rd		In front line - right sector of Divl front. Left outpostn of Bde front. Situation quiet.	Ry Ret. MORBECQUE LA BASSEE 1/10,000 Rec.
"	4th		Unit relieved by 1/6th LANCASHIRE FUSs. On relief unit moved into Support Batt HQ at A 14 a 9/7	Ry 1:25 1:20:60 1/12/17 Ref 1/10,000 36c NW 1 BB
"	5th/8th		Unit in support. Capt E.B. Michaelis proceeded on 10 days leave to ENGLAND on the 5th Lieut R. Alderson M.C. rejoined from " " " Strength of unit on 9th off 43 O.R. 681 - present with unit 30 off 525 O.R. - detailed 11 off 156 O.R.	RRR
"	10th		¼ 126th INF BDE relieved 125th INF BDE - Unit was relieved by 1/5 Batt EAST LANCs REGT. On relief 125 BDE moved into Divl RESERVE, the unit being stationed in OBLINGHEM	Ry 1:25 BDE 2061:9 6:2 6x8/12/17 Ry Ret BETHUNE 1/40,000 RRR

Army Form C. 2118.

WAR DIARY
of
INTELLIGENCE SUMMARY. { 1st/9th Lancashire Fusiliers

(Erase heading not required.)

Instructions regarding War Diaries and Intelligence
Summaries are contained in F. S. Regs., Part II.
and the Staff Manual respectively. Title pages
will be prepared in manuscript.

Place	Date	Hour	Summary of Events and Information	Remarks and references to Appendices
	Dec/17			
OBLINGHEM	11th/21st		During period in Reserve Training was carried out. 2nd Lt Lofting J.H. and 2Lt G Massey joined the unit for duty from England on the 8th and 2Lt H Appleton on 10th. Lt/Col C.G. Jacob proceeded to England to be transferred to the R.F.C. on the 9th. Lieut H.N. Sturt rejoined from 14 days leave in England on 11th. Capt R.G. Byrd " " 28 " " " 12th. Hon Lt O Gen J. Robinson " 18 " " " 13th. Capt E Fairhurst and Capt G.W. Sutton proceeded on 14 days leave to England on 10th. 125 Inf Bde relieved 129 Inf Bde in the Div Left Sector. The unit relieved 1/6th Manchester Regt in the front line in Bde Left Sector. The Portuguese Ex Force was on left flank. 2nd Lt Broadbent proceeded to Base to be transferred to Prisoners of War Coy. Capt E.B. Michaelis rejoined from leave in England.	193
"	22nd		in front line.	4/125 Bde
"	23rd/27th		2Lt J H Lofting wounded 24th " H Appleton " 24th to Hospital Aire 24th	100.63.64 18/19/12/17 R. Maje DIETHUNG/40330 LA BASSÉE RICHEBAURG 5/10/17 R9.B
"	28/31		Unit relieved by 1/6 Lanc Fus. On relief unit moved to Reserve in GORRE on 28th. In Reserve of 41 or bbg - detail 10 of 16 or Strength of unit	4/125 Bde 100.65 25/14/17 R.9.B

OH D Darvel
Lt Col
Comd 1/8 Lan. Fus.

CONFIDENTIAL.

WAR DIARY

of

1/8ᵗʰ Lancashire Fusiliers.

From: 1.1.18.   To: 31.1.18.

Volume 33.

WAR DIARY or INTELLIGENCE SUMMARY

Army Form C. 2118.

Place	Date	Hour	Summary of Events and Information	Remarks and references to Appendices
GORRE	Jan 1st 1918		The Battalion spent New Years Day in billets at GORRE CHATEAU whilst in Brigade Reserve. Fine weather, nothing particular to report.	REF. MAP FRANCE SHEET 36.B
	Jan 2nd 1918		On January 2nd 1918 MAJOR A.L.B. SHAW proceeded to ENGLAND on Senior Officers Course at ALDERSHOT. MAJOR McBIRD took over duties as Second in command of Battalion.	
GORRE to FESTUBERT	Jan 3rd 1918		Battalion moved up into the line and relieved 16th LANCASHIRE FUSILIERS in left Sub section of 125 Brigade in front of FESTUBERT. No. of men on parade.	REF. BATT. OO NO. 66.
FESTUBERT			GORRE CHURCH. The relief being carried out during the day. "A" "B" & "D" Companies being in the line from S.28.a.4.9 to A.3.a.92 and "C" Coy in support Aid SHEETS	REF. MAP FRANCE SHEETS 36 + 36B REF. FRANCE SHEETS 36 + 36B

WAR DIARY or INTELLIGENCE SUMMARY

Army Form C. 2118.

Place	Date	Hour	Summary of Events and Information	Remarks and references to Appendices
ESTRÉ BLANCHE	Jan. 3rd 1918		During the four arrangements when Bn. was into defected [billets?] was carried out. Also the winning of these batteries on the 2nd Jan. 1918. Capt. L.H. Smith was appointed to replace Lieut. B.A. Hinkers proceeded on 14 days leave to England.	
IN THE LINE	Jan. 6th 1918		Lieut. Colonel O. St. L. DAVIES took temporary command of 125 Inf. Brigade. Major M.C. BIRD took command of Battalion. Capt. & Adjt. E. FAIRHURST & Capt. G.W. SUTTON returned from 8 am. to ENGLAND	
	Jan. 9th 1918		2nd/Lieut. J.H. RICK accidentally [killed?] by the explosion of a rifle grenade. All ranks paid the deepest	

WAR DIARY or INTELLIGENCE SUMMARY

Army Form C. 2118.

Place	Date	Hour	Summary of Events and Information	Remarks and references to Appendices
GIVENCHY	Jan 9th 1918		Lieut Col. O.S.R.L. DAVIES rejoined from 125th Brigade and took over command of Battalion. Relieved in the front line by 1/6th LANCASHIRE FUSILIERS and went into the support. A + B Companies into KEEPS of GIVENCHY, C Company A=B=Y D Company in WINDY CORNER AREA.	REF BATT. ORDER NO. 67
				REF MAP SKETCH SHEET 36 c
	Jan 14th 1918		Battalion found working parties. Whilst at WORKS on the am [illeg] 19.1.18 2/Lt GIBBS and RE BIRD were [illeg] 2/28 Bde HQrs as Guides [illeg] shell holes	[signature]
	Jan 24th 1918		Battalion was relieved in support line by 1/4th EAST LANCASHIRE REGT and went into REST. Companies were distributed in huts in NOUVELLE LOBLINGHEN and LE QUESNOY areas E.	REF MAP FRANCE SHEETS 1:36A 36 & 36c 1:50000 AgNo

WAR DIARY or INTELLIGENCE SUMMARY

Army Form C. 2118.

Place	Date	Hour	Summary of Events and Information	Remarks and references to Appendices
GIVENCHY	Jan 17th 1918		Lieut K.B. STORT died from gas poisoning caused by Coke fumes in dug out. 2nd Lieut J.K. RICK returned from hospital.	
OBINGHEN	Jan 18th 1918		Returned unit to Obinghem from Jan 17 1918. Battalion in rest billets at Obinghem finding working parties for the line in advance of the Battalion carrier.	
	Jan 19th 1918		In advance of training.	
	Jan 20th 1918		Lieut W.A. STRUTHERS returned from leave to ENGLAND.	
OBINGHEN	Jan 21st 1918		Capt F.S. BEDALE R.A.M.C. T.F. rejoined Battalion from England took over duties as Medical Officer from Lieut A.W. DICKINSON American Red Cross Medical Officer who returned to 1/5th E. Lancs Field Ambulance	

WAR DIARY or INTELLIGENCE SUMMARY

Army Form C. 2118.

Place	Date	Hour	Summary of Events and Information	Remarks and references to Appendices
OBLINGHEM	JAN 22ND 1918		Bathalem training in most British troops. Country runs and football in the afternoons to JAN 25th 1918 about training in the morning as canal work.	
OBLINGHEM	JAN 26th 1918		A working party of 1 off and 60 O.R. from "A" Coy relieved a similar party of 18th K. LANCAS HIRE FUSILIERS attached to 3rd AUSTRALIAN TUNNELLING COY at CAMBRIN.	Bath 0.0 No 60 REF conference Sheet BETHUME 1/40,000 No 11
	JAN 27th 1918		Major M.G. BIRD and CAPTAIN WM. STOWE proceeded on 14 days leave to ENGLAND. 2nd LIEUT. W.H. TAYLOR returned from 1st ARMY Signal Course.	
OBLINGHEM	JAN 28th 1918		An advance party of 1 officer per company proceeded to the line and to reconnoitre until their companies arrived	Ref 90 No 29

WAR DIARY
or
INTELLIGENCE SUMMARY.

(Erase heading not required.)

Army Form C. 2118.

Place	Date	Hour	Summary of Events and Information	Remarks and references to Appendices
OBSINGHEM & in the LINE	JAN. 29th 1918		Battalion relieved 15th Manchester Regt in left Sub Sector of the Canal Sector front of Givenchy on either side the AIRE-LA BASSÉE CANAL. The relief was felt by all four companies being in the front line. Dispositions being :- D. Company from A90.91 to A15.L.9.8., A15.L.9.8., A15.L.9.11. A15.L.9.8 to A15.L.5.9.11. B Company from A15.L.59 SHEETS to the AIRE-LA BASSÉE CANAL A Company from the AIRE-LA BASSÉE CANAL to A"C" COMPANY from the CANAL to the BRICKSTACKS in front of Givenchy.	REF. BATT. O.O. No. 70. REF. MAP FRANCE A15.L.59 SHEETS 36A 36B
in the line	JAN. 30th 1918		2nd Lieut G. MASON was killed on the morning of the 30th while moving round the line with the Company officer.	
	JAN. 31st 1918		The strength of the Battalion on 31st JAN 1918 was with the Battalion 25 officers 2 P.S.O.R. Detached 11 officers 206 O.R.	

WAR DIARY
or
INTELLIGENCE SUMMARY.

(Erase heading not required.)

Army Form C. 2118.

Place	Date	Hour	Summary of Events and Information	Remarks and references to Appendices
IN THE LINE	Jan 31st 1918		Total Strength of Battalion including attached 36 Officers 689 O.R.	W.J.

D.K. Munn Lt. Col.
Comdg. 2/8th Bn. Lancashire Fusiliers Regt.

SECRET.   COPY NO.............

OPERATION ORDERS NO 66.   2/1/18.

Reference Sheet BETHUNE 1/40.000. LA BASSEE & RICHEBOURG.
1/10.000

---

1. 1/8th. Lancashire Fusiliers will relieve 1/6th Lancashire Fus. in the front line in the left sub-sector on the 3rd instant.

   Dispositions as before with the following exceptions :-
   "D" Coy in Left Front.
   "C" Coy in Support.
   O.C. "D" Coy will arrange with O.C. "C" Coy for N.C.Os. who know the night detached posts. They will be attached for 24 hours. Snipers will be attached to companies as before. The relief of the Lewis Gun Team in FESTUBERT will take place at 9 a.m. by the 5th. L.F. The N.C.O. in charge will have written instructions to rejoin "D" Coy leaving their packs, etc at Battn H.Q. to be sent down the line at night.

2. HOUR AND ORDER OF MARCH   -   "B" Coy. 9. 15 a.m.
                                   "A" "   9. 25 a.m.
                                   "D" "   9. 35 a.m.
                                   "C" "   9. 45 a.m.
                                   H. Q."   10. 0. a.m.

3. STARTING POINT.   -   GORRE CHURCH.   200 yards between platoons will be maintained. Lewis Gun limbers will be loaded tonight - half limber per company. Lewis Gun boxes and ammunition boxes will not be taken up. 24 magazines per gun will be taken up. These 2 limbers with a party of 4 Lewis Gunners per company will start at 8. 45 a.m.. They will be unloaded at Estaminet Corner ready for the companies to pick up.

4. There will be no guides.

5. Watches will be synchronised by the Signal Officer at 5 p.m. today.

6. Relief complete will be notified to Battn H.Q. by code word FIZZ.

7. A C K N O W L E D G E.

Issued at .... p.m.

                                                   Capt.,
                                        A/adjt., 1/8th. Lancashire Fus

Copies to.
No 1. C.O.
   2. 2i/c.
   3. O.C. "A" Coy.
   4. O.C. "B" "
   5. O.C. "C" "
   6. O.C. "D" "
   7. Lt. Struthers.
   8. 2/Lt. Mason.
   9. Quartermaster.
  10. Transport Officer.
  11. 1/6th. L. F.
  12. Medical Officer.
  13. War diary.
  14.   "   "
  15. File.

ADMINISTRATIVE INSTRUCTIONS ISSUED IN CONJUNCTION WITH
OPERATION ORDERS NO 66. 2/1/18.

1. Transport for the line will be alloted as follows. :-
Half G.S. limber per company to be outside guard 3. p.m.
today and loaded tonight.
1 G.S. limber and Mess cart for Battn H.Q. - The limber will
be loaded with bowls, socks, tailors and shoemakers stores,
dixies, at the Quartermasters Stores and report with the Mess
Cart at Battn H.Q. at 9 a.m. These will march in rear of
H.Q. Coy.

2. Blankets, packs, Officers kits etc, will be stacked by companies
on the football ground. Sgt Harrison will be in charge of
the dump, and the Lewis gun class will act as loading party.

3. Drummers, Pioneers, Police, will return to their companies. Lewis
Gun class remain behind under Sgt Harrison. Candidates for
commissions will be attached to their companies in the line.

4. Arrangements for water, rations etc, will be the same as before.
Sgt Common will be responsible for water in cookhouses.
Sgt Shackleton will be in charge of the drying room.
BARBERS TOOLS. Barbers will take their tools up in the line
and carry on their work there.

Capt.,
A/adjt., 1/8th. Lancashire Fusiliers.

SECRET.   COPY NO. 15

OPERATION ORDERS NO 69.   13/1/18.

Ref BETHUNE combined sheet 1/40.000

1. 1/8th Lancashire Fusiliers will be relieved by the 1/4th. East
   Lancashire Regt in Support on 15/1/18.
   On relief companies will move independently by march route to
   OBLINGHEM via LE QUESNOY and BETHUNE and take over the same billets
   as were occupied when last in rest.
   Distance of 200 yards will be maintained between platoons and
   groups of 4 vehicles East of BEUVRY - LOCON LINE. West of this
   a distance of 500 yards between Battalions.

2. (a) Advance Parties of 1/4th. East Lancs Regt will reconnoitre
   support Battalion Area on 14th inst.   Guides as already detailed
   will report at ESTAMINET CORNER at 11 a.m. and will remain in line
   until arrival of their unit on 15th. inst.
   (b) The following guides will report at a place to be notified
   later at 1 p.m. on 15th. to guide companies of 4th. East Lancs
   Regt. which will relieve corresponding companies of 1/8th.
   Lancashire Fusiliers.
          1 guide per platoon.
          1   "   " Coy H.Q.
          1   "   " Lewis Gun A.A. position - "C" Coy.
          2   "   " Battalion H.Q.
   Each guide will be given written instructions showing which
   company, platoon etc he is guide for.

3. All trench stores, Lewis Gun A.A. positions, maps, defence schemes,
   schemes of work and wiring in progress and documents relating
   to this sector, will be handed over on relief. Receipts will
   be forwarded to Battn H.Q. within 24 hours of relief.

4. Orders re Working Parties will be issued later.

5. Relief complete will be notified to Battn H.Q. by code word
   "ENOS".

6. A C K N O W L E D G E.

   Issued at......10......p.m.

                                                    Capt.,
                                  Adjt., 1/8th. Lancashire Fusiliers.

COPIES TO.
No 1.   C.O.
 " 2.   2 i/c.
 " 3.   O.C. "A" Coy.
 " 4.   "   "B" "
 " 5.   "   "C" "
 " 6.   "   "D" "
 " 7.   2/Lieut Mason.
 " 8.   Rear H.Q.
 " 9.   Quartermaster.
 "10.   Transport Officer.
 "11.   1/4th. East. Lanc Regt.
 "12.   Medical Officer.
 "13 & 14 War Diary.
 "15.   FILE.

ADMINSTRATIVE INSTRUCTIONS ISSUED IN CONJUNCTION
WITH O.O. 69.   13/1/18.

1. (a) half limber per "A" "B" and "D" Coys and half limber and maltese and mess carts per Battalion H.Q. will be at WESTMINSTER BRIDGE at 1. 45 p.m. on 15th inst. One limber will report at ESTAMINET CORNER at 1. 45 p.m for use of "C" Coy.
(b) Baggage wagons will report to Transport Lines on evening 14th inst.
One Motor Lorry will be allotted per Battalion. This lorry will be taken over from relieving Battalion of 126th. Bde.

2. Officer i/c Rear H.Q. will arrange for advance billetting parties to proceed to OBLINGHEM to take over billets before unit leaves the area. Guides will meet companies at WINDMILL W. 21.c. 3. 7. on arrival.

3. Rear H.Q. will move under orders of Officer i/c Rear H.Q.

4. Arrangements for baths will be notified later.

Issued as per O.O. 69.

Capt.,
Adjt., 1/8th. Lancashire Fusiliers.

Secret.   Copy No..........

OPERATION ORDER NO 69a.   25/1/18.

Ref. 1/40,000 BETHUNE Combined Sheet.

1. 1 Officer 60 O.R. from "A" Coy will relieve a similar party of 1/6th. Lancashire Fusiliers attached to the 3rd Australian Tunnelling Coy at CAMBRIN tomorrow the 26th inst.

2. HOUR OF MARCH.   9 a.m.
    STARTING POINT.   "A" Coy H.Q.

    The party must not march through BETHUNE, East of a line GORRE - SAILLY - LA BOURSE. 200 yards distance will be maintained between parties of 50 men.

3. 2 limbers will report at "A" Coys H.Q. at 8. 30 a.m. to carry blankets, greatcoats, dixies and officers kit.

4. Men will proceed in fighting order. Packs containing service dress caps will be sent to Q.M.Stores under arrangements to be made by O.C. "A" Coy.

5. Rations for the 26th inst will be taken on limbers.

6. Relief complete will be notified to Battalion H.Q. by code word WORK.

7. A C K N O W L E D G E.

    Issued at............p.m.
                                              Capt.,
                                 Adjt., 1/5th. Lancashire Fusiliers.

Copies to:-

No 1   "A" Coy.
   2. Quartermaster.
   3   Transport Officer.
   4. R. S. M.
   5. Medical Officer.
   6. War Diary.
   7.   "   "
   8. File.

SECRET.   COPY NO. 15

OPERATION ORDERS No 70.   27. 1. 18.

Reference BETHUNE combined sheet. 1/40,000.
          LA BASSEE Sheet.   1/10,000.

1. 1/8th. Lancashire Fusiliers will relieve 1/5th. Manchester Regt, in the left sub-sector of the CANAL SECTOR on 29th inst. in accordance with attached march table.

2. Advance parties of 1 Officer per company, 1 from Battn H.Q. and 1 N.C.O. per platoon will proceed to the line on 28th. inst. and remain until their companies arrive.   Party will rendezvous at Battn H.Q. at 7. 30 a.m.   Guides will meet at PONT FIXE A. 14 c at 11 a.m.

3. All trench stores, A.A.Lewis Gun positions, defence schemes, aeroplane photographs, sketches, schemes of work, in progress, proposed work and working parties will be taken over on relief. Lists of trench stores taken over will be sent to Battn H.Q. within 24 hours of relief.

4. Working Party of 1 Officer and 60 O.R. from "A" Coy will be relieved by similar party of 1/7th. Manchester Regt by 10. 30 a.m. 29th inst. On relief this party will meet guides at PONT FIXE as per attached march table.

5. In the event of the 29th inst being a very bright day relief will be postponed as shown in attached march table.

6. Transport will move immediately in rear of the leading platoon of each company.

7. Completion of relief will be reported to Battn H.Q. by code word "SQUASH".

8. A C K N O W L E D G E.

   Issued at................p.m.

                                                           Capt.,
                                      Adjt., 1/8th. Lancashire Fusiliers.

COPIES TO.
No 1. C.O.
   2. 2 i/c.
   3. O.C. "A" Coy.
   4. O.C. "B" "
   5. O.C. "C" "
   6. O.C. "D" "
   7. Lieut Struthers.
   8. Quartermaster.
   9. Transport Officer.
  10. R. S. M.
  11. O i/c Signals.
  12. Medical Officer.
  13. 1/5th. Manchester Regt.
  14. War Diary.
  15. "   "
  16. File.

ADMINISTRATIVE INSTRUCTIONS ISSUED
IN ACCORDANCE WITH O.O. 70.   27. 1. 18.

1. REFILLING POINT. — No change.

2. TRANSPORT AND BAGGAGE. Baggage wagon will report to Transport lines by 7 a.m. on 29th inst.

   (a) If motor transport is available on 29th inst one motor lorry will report to transport lines at 7 a.m.

   (b) In the event of the present restrictions being in force on 29th inst. Supply wagons will report with the baggage wagons. G.S. Wagons will never move empty.

   (c) Supplies will be drawn by 1st line transport.

   (d) One limber per company, mess cart, maltese cart, and 1 limber per Battn H.Q. will be allotted for the move. Transport will report at respective Headquarters one hour before hour of march.

   (e) All baggage not for the line will be stacked at Quartermaster's Stores by 8. 30 a.m. 29th. inst.

   (f) Transport Lines and Rear H.Q. will move to LE QUESNOY and take over accommodation from 1/5th. Manchester Regt.

3. MOBILE RESERVE. The Quartermaster will arrange to exchange mobile reserve of S.A.A. etc,.

4. GUARDS. The two guards supplied by "A" Coy at present doing duty in BETHUNE will be relieved by 127 Brigade at 11 a.m. 30th inst.

5. LEAVE. A G.S. Limber will leave 1/5th. Lancashire Fusiliers transport lines daily at 9. 30 a.m. commencing 30th inst to convey packs and blankets of men proceeding on leave.

6. DRYING ROOM. Sgt Common will take over Drying Room at PONT FIXE.

7. INDENTS. Indents for R.E. material must reach Battn H.Q. by 7 a.m. daily.

8. RATION DUMPS. (1) Junction of DAWSON STREET and Harley St for Battn H.Q. and "C" Coy.
               (2) Drying Room PONT FIXE for "A" "B" "D" Coys.
Companies will provide their own ration carrying parties with the exception of "C" Coy whose ration party will be provided by "A" Coy. Rations will arrive daily at 5. 15 p.m.

9. TRENCH FOOT CENTRE. Trench Foot Centre near CUINCHY STATION A 14 c 30 65. is allotted as per attached table. Rate 40 men per hour. Full value must be taken as far as possible of the Trench Foot Centre.

ISSUED AS PER O.O. 70.

                                Capt.,
                   Adjt., 1/8th. Lancashire Fusiliers.

Hq C.D.A.B.

March Table to accompany O.D. 70

Order of March :- Hq. C.D.A.B. Group

Unit No.	Unit	From	To Relieve	Route	Allow it Water	Hour of travel of bright day	Meeting Point	Garden meet	Garden meet if bright day
1	Working Party (A Coy, 1 off 1 box)	CAMBRIN	C Coy 5th Wels. Regt.	Boot route to Pont Fixe Walmunster Bridge	—			Pont Fixe 11:30 am	Pont Fixe 3:30 pm
2	A Coy LQ	OBINGHEM	C Coy 5th Wels. Regt.						
3	B Coy	ditto	A Coy ditto	Béthune Rd. E15c to 3.—	9:30 am	10:30 pm	Railway Crossing N.26b 00	Walmunster Bridge F18a 11:30 am	Walmunster Bridge F18a 3:30 pm
4	C Coy	ditto	D Coy ditto	E11d. H.9.- Northern Avent Park					
5	D Coy	ditto	B Coy ditto						
6	Batt. H.Q.	ditto	5th Wels. Regt.						

Note. 10 intervals of 200 yards will be maintained between platoons on the march.

Geo. Parkinson Capt.
Adjt. 1/5th Lan. Fusiliers

27.1.18

125/42

Vol 13

32. N.
8 sheets

CONFIDENTIAL

War Diary
of
1/8th Lancashire Fusiliers.

From 1/2/18 to 28/2/18

Volume 34.

WAR DIARY
or
INTELLIGENCE SUMMARY.   1st/8th Lancashire Fusiliers

(Erase heading not required.)

Army Form C. 2118.

Instructions regarding War Diaries and Intelligence Summaries are contained in F. S. Regs., Part II. and the Staff Manual respectively. Title pages will be prepared in manuscript.

Place	Date	Hour	Summary of Events and Information	Remarks and references to Appendices
IN THE LINE	1st/2nd Feb 1918	—	Unit in the front line in front of CUINCHY. A patrol went out on night of 1st/2nd to the derelict enemy aeroplane which had been brought down by A.A. fire on the 31st ult. They brought back the machine gun and other fittings after the aeroplane 2Lt. J.C.T. TOONER reported missing. He went out into "No Man's Land" alone & apparently lost his way.*	By RAD LA BASSÉE 1/10,000 *Reported prisoner in German hands 22/2/18 ROS
LA BASSÉE CANAL SECTOR				
IN SUPPORT	3rd		Unit relieved by 1/6th Lanc Fus⁰ & on relief moved back into Support Batt HQ at A 20 b 8.3.	By 125 Bde 00/01.2.18 ROS
"	4th/7th		In Support. Working parties to the front line found each night.	
IN THE LINE	8th/13th		Unit relieved 1/6th Lanc Fus⁵ in front line on the 8th. Situation quiet throughout the tour. Lieut J WHITE rejoined from 14 days leave in UK on arriving detailed on 42 Div H.Q. Lieut S.A. SPRINGBETT & party of 20 O.R. rejoined from attachment to 427 Cy RE on 11.2.18.	By 125 Bde 00 71.5.2.18 ROS
"	14th		The 125th Inf Bde was relieved by the 164th Inf Bde on the 14th. Unit relieved by 1/4 Loyal North Lanc Reg⁺ On relief unit moved into reserve area into VAUDRICOURT.	By 125 Bde 00 92 R BETHUNE Gen Sheet 1/40,000

WAR DIARY
INTELLIGENCE SUMMARY. 1/8th LANCASHIRE FUSILIERS

Army Form C. 2118.

Place	Date	Hour	Summary of Events and Information	Remarks and references to Appendices
VAUDRICOURT	15th/20th		Training carried out.	Ry BETHUNE D Sheet Con^d V40,000
	15/2/18		Capt. W.M. STONE rejoined from 14 days leave in U.K.	
	16/2/18		The following officers joined the unit from the 1/6th LANC FUS. 1st r-unit being disbanded.	
			Capt. A H LAWE, 2nd Lieut. S. CLAY, J.H. LISTER, F. ORMEROD, W. MARSHALL & J.G. LYNER	RB
	18/2/18		Lieut H.B. IVERS admitted to hospital sick	
	21/28		Training continued.	
	22/2/18		2Lt H TRICKETT joined the unit from the LABOUR CORPS as reinforcement.	
	23/2/18		Major M.G. BIRD rejoined unit from leave in U.K.	
	26/2/18		2Lt F. ORMEROD admitted to hospital sick	
	28/2/18		Lieut T. WHITE rejoined unit from 42 Div H.Q.	
			The following reinforcements joined the unit during the month. 10/2/18 6 of 130 OR (from 1/6 LF disbanded)	
			19/2/18 - 27 OR : 23/2/18 - 84 OR. 20/2/18 - 22 OR. 25/2/18 - 45 OR. 29/2/18 - 17 O.R.	
			Strength of unit on 28th :- Offs 41, OR 890 : Detailed offs 14, O.R. 195.	

O.W. Meunier Lt Col
Com^g 1/8 LANC FUS
28/2/18

42nd Division.
125th Infantry Brigade.

1/8th BATTALION

LANCASHIRE FUSILIERS

MARCH 1 9 1 8

CONFIDENTIAL

WAR DIARY

of

1/8th LANCASHIRE FUSILIERS

From 1-3-18   To 31-3-18

VOLUME 35.

Army Form C. 2118.

WAR DIARY
of
INTELLIGENCE SUMMARY. 1/8TH LANCASHIRE FUSILIERS.

(Erase heading not required.)

Instructions regarding War Diaries and Intelligence Summaries are contained in F. S. Regs., Part II. and the Staff Manual respectively. Title pages will be prepared in manuscript.

Place	Date	Hour	Summary of Events and Information	Remarks and references to Appendices
VAUDRICOURT. REF. MAP. BETHUNE 1/40,000	MARCH 1918. 1st/22nd		During this period training was carried out in the Unit, consisting of Close Order Drill, Musketry, and Tactical Training by Platoons and Companies. The afternoon of each day was devoted to Recreational Training.	Ins.
REF. MAPS. BETHUNE 1/40,000 LENS. No 11. 1/100,000	23rd		Division moved to ADINFER. The Unit moved by Train to ADINFER, entraining at 10.30 a.m. from FOUQUIERES - LABUISSIERE ROAD J.5.d.3.2, and bivouaced for the night in the wood at ADINFER. Transport moved by road via HAILLICOURT - HOUDAIN, under orders of the Bde. TRANSPORT OFFICER.	REF. 125. INF. BDE. O.O. No 75 Ins.
SHEET 57cNW 1/20,000	24th		125th. BDE. relieved the 120th. INF. BDE. in the line, moving by day to a position of readiness in LOGEAST WOOD (A.25.central). The relief was carried out by night, the Unit Taking over positions in support to 1/5th. + 1/7th. LANCS. FUS. who occupied the front line which was roughly as follows:- (B.30.c.8.6). (B.29.c.8.9) (B.29.a.4.8) (B.28.b.0.4) (B.28.a.0.4). The Unit, which relieved the 1/7th. EAST SURREYS was disposed in squares:- (H.5.b) (H.4.a) (B.27.d).	REF. 125.INF.BDE. WIRE:- B.M. 105. Ins.

Army Form C. 2118.

WAR DIARY
INTELLIGENCE SUMMARY.
(Erase heading not required.)

1/8th LANCASHIRE FUSILIERS.

Place	Date	Hour	Summary of Events and Information	Remarks and references to Appendices
REF. MAP SHEET 57 M.M 1/20,000	MARCH 1918 25th		Heavy fighting all day during which the Battalion, which was in support to 1/5th Lancs. Fus. + 1/7th Lancs. Fus., moved forward and made an attack capturing the villages of SAPIGNIES and BEHAGNIES. About 2.30 p.m. the 125' I. Bde was forced to withdraw to the GOMMIECOURT RIDGE, due to the flanks giving way. The Battalion then occupied positions in A 30 d and G 6 b. For a time the enemy was held up, but at 2 p.m. on the 26th inst. the 125' I. Bde. was again forced to withdraw. The Battalion suffered the following officer casualties during the 25th inst:— MAJOR. M.G. BIRD (C.O) wounded. CAPT E.B. MICHAELIS wounded. CAPT. A. HALLAWELL wounded. CAPT. R. ALDERSON M.C. died of wounds. CAPT. E.G. SPEAKMAN wounded. LIEUT. W.H. STRUTHERS wounded. 2/LIEUT E.G. SPEAKMAN wounded. 2/LIEUT A. STANDING wounded. 2/LIEUT. G. MASSEY wounded + missing (believed prisoner.) 2/LIEUT A. LANGDON wounded. O.R. Casualties estimated at 210.	J.T.

Army Form C. 2118.

WAR DIARY
INTELLIGENCE SUMMARY.
(Erase heading not required.)

1st/8th LANCASHIRE FUSILIERS.

Place	Date	Hour	Summary of Events and Information	Remarks and references to Appendices
SHEET 57°N.E. 1/20,000	MARCH 1918 26th/27th		After withdrawal the Battalion took up a position near ABLAINZEVELLE which was held for some time, but it was found necessary to withdraw further to a position East of ESSARTS. Here the 125 I.Bde withdrew in support to the 42nd Division which held a line from AYETTE to ABLAINZEVELLE. During this time the Battalion was in a position - F20 a & c.	July.
do.	28th		The 125 I.Bde relieved the 185 I.Bde and part of the 127 I.Bde in the line on the night of the 28th inst. The battalion relieved 2 Coys of 2/5th WEST YORKS and 2 Coys 8th WEST YORKS in support in square F26 c & d.	REF 125 I.Bde Message BM.156. July.
do.	29th/31st		The 125 I.Bde was relieved in the line by the 124th I.Bde on the night of the 29th inst. and on relief occupied positions in the GOMMECOURT LINE. The battalion was relieved by the 2/7th WEST SURREYS and on relief occupied positions in the right front of the above line extending from K5d67 to E29 621.	REF 125 I.Bde Message BM.153. July.

James S. MacLeod
Major
1st/8th Lancashire Fusiliers

125th Inf.Bde.
42nd Div.

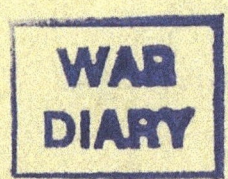

1/8th BATTN. THE LANCASHIRE FUSILIERS.

A P R I L

1 9 1 8

CONFIDENTIAL

WAR DIARY

of

1/8 LANCASHIRE FUSILIERS.

From 1.4.18   To 30.4.18

VOLUME 36.

Army Form C. 2118.

WAR DIARY
or INTELLIGENCE SUMMARY.
(Erase heading not required.)

1/8TH LANCASHIRE FUSILIERS.

Place	Date	Hour	Summary of Events and Information	Remarks and references to Appendices
SHEET 57 D. NE 1/20,000	APRIL 1918. 1st / 2nd		The 125 I. Bde. together with 1/7 N.F. Pioneers relieved the 124 I. Bde. and 1 Bn. of the 122 I. Bde. in the line on the night of the 1st inst. The 1/8 L.F. Bn. relieved the 20th D.L.I. from Right Boundary L.3.d.91 to Road inclusive L.4.a.66 — H. Qrs. at F.26.d.00.	REF. 125 I. Bde Message BM.178. *Sgd*
do.	3rd / 6		The Battalion relieved 5 platoons of the 1/7 N.F. Pioneers between limits L.4.a.66 and the grid line between squares F.28 & L.4 on the night of the 3rd inst. At 5 A.M. on the 5th inst. the enemy put down a heavy barrage for three hours. He attacked at 9 A.M. and drove in the left flank. The 1/7th LANCS. FUS. formed a defensive flank. The right flank held out but was afterwards forced to withdraw through village of BUCQUOY. The remnants of the battalion, consisting of 80 men, in conjunction with the 1/5th LANCS. FUS. counter-attacked about 4.30 P.M. and re-established a line somewhat in rear of our original position. The Battalion suffered the following Officer casualties during	REF. 125 I. Bde Message BM.198. *Sgd*

WAR DIARY
INTELLIGENCE SUMMARY

1/8 LANCASHIRE FUSILIERS

Army Form C. 2118.

Place	Date	Hour	Summary of Events and Information	Remarks and references to Appendices
	APRIL 1918			
SHEET 57D-N.E 1/20000	7th		The 5th inst.— T/Lt.Col. O.St.L. DAVIES, killed. CAPT. G.W. SUTTON, wounded. LIEUT. H. THRUSH, missing. LIEUT. H.B. IVERS, wounded. 2/LIEUT. A.C. GIBBONS, wounded. 2/LIEUT. J.H. RICK, missing. 2/LIEUT. J.G. LYMER, missing. 2/LIEUT. E.W. ROSE, killed. 2/LIEUT. L.J. CLAY, killed. O.R. casualties estimated at 202.	S&J.
LENS SHEET N 1/100000	8th/12th		The 125 I Bde. was relieved in the line by the 185 I Bde and part of the 186 I Bde. on the night of the 7th inst., and on relief went into CORPS RESERVE. The Battalion, which was in support in the YELLOW LINE immediately N. of the ESSARTS-BUCQUOY Rd. was relieved by part of the 2/7th WEST YORKS REGT. and on relief marched to SOUASTRE and from there proceeded by bus to billets at VAUCHELLES. During this period the battalion remained in billets at VAUCHELLES. General reorganization and training was carried on.	REF. 125 I Bde order N°75 S&J.
SHEET 57D 1/40000	13th/15th		The 125 I Bde. group, with exception of 1/7 LANCS.FUS. moved on the 13th inst. via AUTHIE to Trévenos in WARNIMONT WOOD, the Battalion leaving starting point at 4.16 AM. Reorganization and training was continued.	REF. 125 I BDE order N°76 S&J.

WAR DIARY
INTELLIGENCE SUMMARY. 1/8 - LANCASHIRE FUSILIERS.

Army Form C. 2118.

(Erase heading not required.)

Place	Date	Hour	Summary of Events and Information	Remarks and references to Appendices
SHEET 57 D 1 H0000	APRIL 1918 16th 17th		The 125 I BDE. relieved the 112 I BDE. in Centre of Divnl. Sector on nights 16th and 17th inst. The Battalion relieved the 6th BED. REGT on the Left of 112 I BDE. Front on the night of the 16th inst. – H.Qrs at K5 d 98.	REF. 125 I BDE ORDER No 77
SHEET 57 D - NE. 1 20000	25th		On the night of the 24th inst. the 125 I BDE extended their right front to K10 d 43, and the Battalion took over from 1/5 7th LANCS. FUS. down to K11 d 10.65.	REF. 125 I BDE ORDER No 78
do.	26th /28th		On the night of the 25th inst. the 1/5 K EAST LANCS. REGT. took over that portion of the line held by the Battalion down to K6 c 20.35.

On the nights of the 26th, 27th and 28th inst. the Battalion owing to information obtained through capable Patrols, pushed forward and occupied a series of posts on a front of 700 yards laterally, and 500 yards deep (approx.) Position occupied K6 c 9.1. – K11 B 15. – K11 B 17. The position was maintained. | REF. 125 I BDE Instructions L.7. 24/4/18 Sgd. |
| do. | 29th /30th | | The 125 I BDE. was relieved in the line by the 127 I BDE. on the night of the 28th inst. The Battalion was relieved by the 1/6th MAN. REGT. and on relief proceeded by the ROSSIGNOL FARM, taking over route to Divisional Reserve. from 1/5 7th MAN. REGT. in

Battalion in billets at ROSSIGNOL FARM. James S. MacLeod Lt Col. Commg. 1/8 LANCS. FUSILIERS | REF. 125 I BDE ORDER No 79 Sgd. Sgd. |

CONFIDENTIAL 125/24

WAR DIARY

of

1/8th LANCASHIRE FUSILIERS

From 1st.5.18
To 31st.5.18.

VOLUME 37.

WAR DIARY

INTELLIGENCE SUMMARY - 1/8TH LANCS FUSILIERS.

Army Form C. 2118.

(Erase heading not required.)

Place	Date	Hour	Summary of Events and Information	Remarks and references to Appendices
ROSSIGNOL FARM 1/20000 57D.N.E.	May 1916	2 AM	Battn in billets at ROSSIGNOL FARM. Relieved 1/5th East Lancashire Regt in Left Sector :- "A" & "B" Coys in FRONTLINE "C" Coy in Support "D" Coy in Reserve. Bn HQ. K.6.A.2.2. Relief complete without incident.	Ref 1/20000 57D.N.E Order No 72.
Ref 1/20000 57D.N.E. K.6.A.2.2.	3rd		Quiet day without incident.	
	4th	7 pm	Battalion shelled in Left Sector. Battn also in a position to front line Bombers. During the night our Sqts issued 1502 Gamete on Right.	Ref 125 2nt Batt Order L.15 + NO 81.
	5th	6 AM	Battn relieved by 2/7 KINGS LIVERPOOL Regt and took over camp in COUIN WOOD. Heavy rain throughout the night and intense darkness increased difficulties of relief - Last parties not arriving in camp until 6 A.M.	Ref 1/25000 Order No 82.
COUIN WOOD	7th		Rifle inspection relieved up. Rain.	
- do -	8th		Clean up and training - fine weather.	
- do -	9th		Divisional sister to "Practice Battle Position". Battn Left Camp at 9 AM returning at 4 pm.	
- do -	10th		Training and inspection camp. Fine and Sunny.	
- do -	11th		Dull day. "Practice Battle Position" Ordered at 7.15 AM. Battalion moved off from Camp within an hour.	
- do -	12th		Brigade Church Parade. 1 Coy on works party.	

Army Form C. 2118.

WAR DIARY
or
INTELLIGENCE SUMMARY. 1/8th LANCS FUSILIERS.
(Erase heading not required.)

Place	Date	Hour	Summary of Events and Information	Remarks and references to Appendices
COOIN WOOD 57 D N E. 1/20,000	MAY 14/5	13th	Training and ceremonial parade. 1 Coy on Working Party. Heavy Rain.	
— " —	14/5 to 28/5		During this period training and carrying on consisted of Rifle and Gas Drill, Musketry, Tactics in the field and by Sections, Platoons and Company's. Three "Gas" lectures to each Battalion. Gas Drill and lecture on being shelled. Individual Turnout, Platoon Competitions were carried out. A Divisional Boxing Tournament was also arranged, being held at PAS on the 27th, 28th and 29th. The 8th Lancs Medals won by Silver Cup presented by Major General Solly Flood C.M.G. D.S.O., tied to best boxing unit in the Division.	
— " —	29th			
— " —	30th		Training. 2 Coys on working parade. Presentation of Rittmolls by G.O.C. Division.	
— " —	31st		Three Coys Training one Company on working party. C & D Coys carried out range practice. Fine and dry.	

James S. MacLeod
Cmdg. 1/8th Bn. Lancashire Fusrs.

CONFIDENTIAL. 125/42

WAR DIARY.

of

1/8th LANCASHIRE FUSILIERS

From 1st. 6. 18.

To 30th. 6. 18.

VOLUME 38.

WAR DIARY

INTELLIGENCE SUMMARY
(Erase heading not required.)

1/8th LANCASHIRE FUSILIERS.

Army Form C. 2118.

Instructions regarding War Diaries and Intelligence Summaries are contained in F. S. Regs., Part II. and the Staff Manual respectively. Title pages will be prepared in manuscript.

Place	Date	Hour	Summary of Events and Information	Remarks and references to Appendices
Ref 57 D NE 1/20000	1/6/18		Training + Bath. 1 Coy on Working Party.	S2y.
J.2.A. 80. 80.	2/6/18		Church Parade.	S2y.
COUIN WOOD	3/6/18		"B" Coy- Working Party. A.C. + D Coys Training, Range practice +c.	S2y.
"	4/6/18		3 Coys Bathing. 1 Coy Working Party.	S2y.
"	5/6/18		Battalion in Attack (practice)	S2y.
"	6/6/18		Bath. moved in two's taking over from 2nd Battn. N.Z. Rifle Bde. in Brigade Reserve at SAILLY-AU-BOIS. J.18.D.6.8. Coming under tactical command of G.O.C. 127 Infantry Bde.	S2y.
SAILLY AU BOIS	7/6/18 to 15/6/18		Battalion remained in Brigade Reserve until the night of 14/15 June. On the morning of 8th inst "B" Coys moved their positions relieving B + D Coys of the 1st WELLINGTON REGT in K.13.2.0. and K.8.C.3.7. respectively. The sector one general trench and saunn. On the night 14/15 June to 155 Infantry Bde. took over from the 127 Infantry Bde. in the Left Divisional Sector. The 1/8 LANCASHIRE FUSILIERS took over from 1/6 Batt. MANCHESTER	S2y.
HEBUTERNE	16/6/18 to 23/6/18		REGT. in Support. Batt. H.Q. at K.9.A. 60.70. Battn. remained in Support until the night of 23rd inst. Weather changeable. Working Parties findrest trenchwit.	

Army Form C. 2118.

WAR DIARY
INTELLIGENCE SUMMARY
of 1/8 LANCASHIRE FUSILIERS

(Erase heading not required.)

Place	Date	Hour	Summary of Events and Information	Remarks and references to Appendices
Ref 57.D.N.E. 1/20000	27/8/19		The Battn moved up into the Left Front Battn. Bats. Sector taking over from the 1/8 LANCASHIRE FUSILIERS. Battn HQrs situated at K.9.D.1.2.	SS.1.
HEBUTERNE	to 30/8/19		The tour in the lines was a particularly quiet one and the weather good. There is nothing of interest to report.	

Lieut Colonel
Commanding 1/8 Lancashire Fusiliers

CONFIDENTIAL.

WAR DIARY

of

1/8 LANCASHIRE FUSILIERS

From 1st. 7. 16.   To 31st. 7. 16.

VOLUME 39.

WAR DIARY

INTELLIGENCE SUMMARY.

Army Form C. 2118.

Sheet 1.

1/8 LANCASHIRE FUSILIERS

Place	Date	Hour	Summary of Events and Information	Remarks and references to Appendices
Ref 57 D N E. 1/26.O.D. HEBUTERNE	1/7/18	—	Quiet day - nothing to report.	P.9.
	2/7/18	—	Quiet day. Battn was relieved by 2 Companies BK 2/2 Batt. NEW ZEALAND RIFLE BDE. After relief Battn HQ. B & D Coys went back in to bivouac in J.22.c. "C" Coy to bivouac at J.28.B.1.5. and A Coy to bivouac at J.23.B.4.3. Relief complete without incident by 1 A.M.	P.9.
BIVOUACS J.22.C. & PURPLE REDERNE	3/7/18 to 9/7/18	—	During this time working parties were supplied for trench digging, laying cable, making Coy training. Training was carried out by Coys incl: musketry, Physical Training, Close order drill, Musketry, with Lewis gun practice and Lewis Gun classes. Recreational training was also organised.	P.9.
— " —	10/7/18	—	Work parties in morning. Afternoon spent in preparing for the relief. Battn started to move up to relieve the 7th MANCHESTER REGT in the left subsector of the Right Sector of the Divisional Front. The relief was completed without incident by 8 p.m. Dispositions after relief :- A & B Coys Right and Left Front, and D & C Coys in Right and Left Support respectively. Battn H.Qrs. K.25.A.8.5. The Line in the Line was a quiet one with the usual periodical concentrations shoots by our artillery on selected targets.	P.9.
COLINCAMPS	11/7/18 to 18/7/18			
Ref. 57 3 N E & S.E. 1/20000	18/7/18 9/7/19		Battn was relieved by the 1/5 LANCASHIRE FUSILIERS — moving back to Support. Battn H.P. at the CORK TRENCH at Q.I.B.0.5. A Coy — BEAUSSART SWITCH, "B" Coy J.30.d.6.2. "C" Coy K.25.d.4.2. "D"Coy CORK TRENCH.	P.9.

Sheet 2.

Army Form C. 2118.

WAR DIARY
or
INTELLIGENCE SUMMARY

(Erase heading not required.) 1/8 LANCASHIRE FUSILIERS.

Place	Date	Hour	Summary of Events and Information	Remarks and references to Appendices
Ref 57 DNE+SE 1/20000	19/7/18 to 26/7/18 Q.1.B.0.5.	—	During this period the Batt. were in Support and carried out Trench Routine and Supplied working parties. There is little Printed Report. Small Raids were carried out on the Brigade front but the Battalion did not participate.	
—	26/27 Night	—	The 125 Infantry Bde was relieved by the 126 Infantry Bde. This Battalion was relieved by the 1/10 Batt. MANCHESTER REG.T and moved back into Divisional Reserve taking over camp at J.20.A.8.0. from 1/5th Batt. KING'S LIVERPOOL Regt. The relief was completed without incident and all men in their Camp by 10 p.m.	S.H.
BUS-LES- ARTOIS Camp at J.20.A.8.O.	28/7/18 to 31/7/18	—	During this period reorganisation and training was carried out. Included Range Practices and Lewis Gun Classes. Two Companies were supplied each day for work - being employed on wiring Trench diggings.	S.H.

W. W. W. Ward MAJOR
Commanding 1/8 Lancs Fusiliers

CONFIDENTIAL

WAR DIARY

of

1/8th LANCASHIRE FUSILIERS

From 1st 8. 18

To 31st 8. 18

VOLUME 40.

WAR DIARY
or
INTELLIGENCE SUMMARY

Army Form C. 2118.

SHEET No. 1

1/8 Lancashire Fusiliers

Place	Date	Hour	Summary of Events and Information	Remarks and references to Appendices
Ref. sq DNE-SE 1/20,000	1/8/18		1/8 Lanc. Fus. in Divisional Reserve in camp at J.20.A.5.0. Murder Day. Practise of musketry	awp
BUS-LES-ARTOIS camp at J.20 A.5.0	2/8/18		by Divisional Commander. 2 boys front working party at COZINCAMPS.	awp
	3/8/18		2 boys front working parties. 2 boys carried out training programme. Battn. moved up and relieved 1/7th Hamps. Regt. in the line. Right Sub. Sect. Support Brigade. Relief all out without incident. Disposit. after relief :- Batt. HQ K19 C 6.0, A Coy in K25 B 10.60, B Coy K27 ex	awp
K19C 6.0	4/8/18		C Coy K21 d 5.4, D Coy K21 b 5.0 Quiet day. Nothing important to report.	awp
	5/8/18		Patrols pushed forward and installed as front in RED COTTAGE K28 a.3.3.	awp
	6/8/18		Daylight patrols sent out to observe movements of enemy when is reported to evacuate some of his forward parts.	awp
	7/8/18		Intra. Coy. relief. A Coy relieving B Coy in front line	awp
	8/8/18		OBSERVATION WOOD, K 28 B, reconnoitred and enemy front line found still installed & then	awp
	9/8/18		Quiet day. Usual artillery harassing of enemy positions.	awp
	10/8/18 to 13/8/18		Usual trench routine. Intra-Coy relief on 12/8/18 C Coy relieving A Coy in front line. Several daylight patrols pushed out many movements.	awp

WAR DIARY or INTELLIGENCE SUMMARY

Army Form C. 2118.

SHEET No 2

1/5 Lancashire Fusiliers

Place	Date	Hour	Summary of Events and Information	Remarks and references to Appendices
Hq 57 DNE and SE	14.8.18		2/Lt E Batty, Killed and 1 O.R. wounded and missing on daylight patrol. Line was advanced during the afternoon to a line running from K 30 d 10 to K 36 d 4.4. The front was carried out in conjunction with 1/7th Lan Fus on the Left and 127 Bde on Right. Posts were established in new line.	awp
	15.8.18		Lines were full on 14.8.18 reconstituted and intensive relief carried out. Bttn HQ at K 19 c 70.00	awp
	16.8.18		Bttn, in engagement with a Coy of 1/7th Lan Fus advanced the line to E 27 c 0.3 – T 26 d 9.0 – E 32 b 7.6	awp
	17.8.18		Heavy Artly bombardt. the Shells in E 26 b – 27 c – 33 a – 32 b from 11.30am to 1pm. On complete of bombardment reconnoitring patrols pushed forward and maintained touch with the enemy.	awp
	18.8.18		Aft. 1 hours bombardment of Shells in E 26 b – 27 c – 33 a – 32 b. B Coy sent out patrols to get in touch with enemy and watch his movement, patrols staying out till 4 a.m. B Coy relieved by A Coy after 4. 18/19/18	awp
	19.8.18		Organisation of new position and observing enemy by patrols	awp
	20.8.18		Preparation for the attack which the 3rd Army has been ordered to make to pierce the enemy front line WEST of BAPAUME. A Coy withdrawn from line under orders from Bde H.Q. and occupied trench WALTER TRENCH in K 29 b and d.	awp

# WAR DIARY or INTELLIGENCE SUMMARY

SHEET No 3   Army Form C. 2118.

1/5 Lancashire Fusiliers

Place	Date	Hour	Summary of Events and Information	Remarks and references to Appendices
Ref. 57D.N.E 1/20,000 57C	21.8.18		1/5 Bttn on Left of Divisional Front. 1/8 Lancs Fus. Battn on Right. Battn H.Q. at Runner. Batt H.Q. at K19 c 6.0. Sent at 3 a.m and reported at K.21 & 69 at the same hour. Zero hour was 4.55 a.m At ZERO plus 12.0 the disposition of 1/8 Lan. Fus. was as follows — Bttn H.Q. K.16.c.4.7., A Coy K.29 b and d, B Coy CETORIX and JEAN BART K.22 A and C, C Coy NORTHERN AVENUE approx K.22.d.-28.b, D Coy ROB ROY TRENCH K.29.a.	aap
	22.8.18		Orders received for plans for days at disposal of O.C. 1/7 Lancs Fus. to carry out an attack. Organised and preparation for the attack.	aap
	23.8.18		A and D Coys detailed to attack two objectives — 1st E.28.c.45.85 – E.28 a 85.10 thence due East E.28.b.95.10 which was consolidated and Rell. 2nd E.34.a.50.70 – E.29.c.00.00. E.29.c.50.55. Zero hour 2.30 a.m. At 3am + 10 troops assaulted and captured 1st Objective. At 3am + 26 2nd Objective Allwas captured and patrols sent out. During this operation 50 prisoners were taken and 8 Machine Guns. Batte was relieved by 1/5 Batte East Lancs. Regt and concentrated near LOUPART WOOD	aap
BEAUREGARD DOVECOTE	24.8.18			aap
	25.8.18		1/5 Bn moved to MIRAUMONT and Bivouac'd on ground WEST of the village	aap
	26.8.18		Recuperating. Training. renewal of clothing, equipment, etc.	aap

WAR DIARY
or
INTELLIGENCE SUMMARY
(Erase heading not required.)

SHEET No. 4   Army Form C. 2118.

1/5 Lancashire Fusiliers

Place	Date	Hour	Summary of Events and Information	Remarks and references to Appendices
M.4 37.C	27.8.18		125th Bde in Rear (Divisional) Battn. moved to M.30.a.30.20 and bivouaced at the spot	app
	28.8.18		Training carried out into Coy. arrangements	app
	29.8.18		Working parties provided for digging and wiring defensive localities	app
	30.8.18			
57c N.W	31.8.18		Battn. relieved 1/7 Manch. Regt. in the line at BRICKFIELDS N.2.a central coming under the tactical command of G.O.C. 127 Bde. On completion of relief defensive area as follows:—	app
57c S.W			BATT'N H.Q. BRICKFIELDS N.2.a central. Area W. of road running N.W. to S.E. in N.2.b.	
			"B" Coy in support to "A" Coy. Area W. of road running N.W. to S.E. in N.3.c.	
			"C" Coy in trench running from N.2 central to N.2.b.6.10	
			"D" Coy in support to "C" Coy in trench running from N.2.c.90.40 to N.2.b.35.25	

James S. Macleod Lieut. Col.
Cody 1/5 Lancashire Fusiliers

CONFIDENTIAL.

175/42

WAR DIARY.

OF

1/8 LANCASHIRE FUSILIERS.

From 1/9/18.   To 30/9/18.

VOLUME 41.

WAR DIARY
INTELLIGENCE SUMMARY.

(Erase heading not required.) 1/8 LANCASHIRE FUSILIERS

Army Form C. 2118.

Sheet 1
September 1918

Place	Date	Hour	Summary of Events and Information	Remarks and references to Appendices
Ref Map Sheet 57.c 1/40000 BRICKFIELDS - N.2.A. THILLOY	1/9/18	—	Battalion remained in position taken up on the night 31/8/18 - 1/9/18. G.O.C. 127 Inf Bde held conference of Battn Commanders suggest concerned in the attack to take place various 2nd inst.	S.M.
— " —	2/9/18 Midday		Moved to vicinity of REINCOURT. VILLERS-AU-FLOS having been taken by 127 Infantry Bde.	S.M.
		12.30 pm.	Battn ordered to be prepared to attack and take the high ground E of VILLERS-AU-FLOS. Instructions were issued by Commandy Officers and assembly positions reconnoitred by Coy Commanders. This attack was cancelled later in the afternoon.	
		5 pm.	Ordered to relieve the 6th Manchesters in the left Sect Bde Div Front.	S.M.
RIENCOURT		8 pm.	Bn H.Qrs at N.5.D.3.1. Relief was hampered owing to the Minny Coy Boundaries being rather vague owing to the fighter of the morning. Relief was complete by 8 A.M.	S.M.
— " —	3/9/18	At 5 pm.	Fighting Patrols were pushed forward to find out where about if the enemy and two hour later on were in occupation of all the high ground East of VILLERS AU FLOS.	S.M.
		8.30 A.M.	Battn ordered to act as advance guard to the Division and to push on through BARASTRE-BUS YTRES and take up line up Bus in trench system East YTRES. The advance was continued throughout the day and by 5 pm. the Battn was disposed in position just West of YTRES with A'D' Coys in Front Line Supported by "B" and "C" Coys. Battn H.Qrs at BUS.	S.M.
BUS	— " —			

WAR DIARY
INTELLIGENCE SUMMARY

Sheet 2

1/8 LANCASHIRE FUSILIERS

Place	Date	Hour	Summary of Events and Information	Remarks and references to Appendices
Ref Map Sheet 57C 1/40000 B.V.S.	3/9/18		A Troop of the Scots Greys were attached to the Battn. for Recce. Skirmishers and did good work by working through at far as LECHELLE. A report sent from here stating that they had come under M.G. fire from LITTLE WOOD was received at Battn. H.Q.rs at B.V.S. at abt 4 p.m. Orders were then sent to them to B.V.S. and assist further instructions. The advance was continued at 5 p.m. by B.T.C.G.S. who passed through A.T.D.C.S. and pushed on to the third objective – the Tunnel System EAST of YTRES – running through P.20.B. – 21.C. – 27.D and 27.D. Truck was obtained with the NEW ZEALAND DIVISION on left and endeavours were made to get truck with the people on its right but this was not obtained until the following morning. B.T.C.G.S. were in position in front objective at 10:30 p.m. but no rest cover for to Battn. H.Q.rs only to heavy hostile gas shelling. At 4 A.M. orders were issued to A.T.D.C.S. to push forward and get into line with B.T.C.G.S. who remained his in position by Battn. H.Q.rs DISTRIBUTED at 6 A.M. to RAILWAY EMBANKMENT in P.20.C. Battn. H.Q.rs moved to AMMUNITION PITS at P.19.B. 20.40.	V.H.
—"—	4/9/18	6 A.M.	During the day the 1/5 LANCS FUSILIERS passed through on line E. of YTRES and we therefore became the supporting Battn.	V.H.
—"—	5/9/18	—	Remained in same position throughout the day. A successful attack was carried out by 1/7th LANCS FUSILIERS this evening.	V.H.

Army Form C. 2118.

WAR DIARY
or
INTELLIGENCE SUMMARY.
(Erase heading not required.)

Army Form C. 2118.

Sheet 3.

Place	Date	Hour	Summary of Events and Information	Remarks and references to Appendices
Ref Map Sheet 57c 1/40,000 PYS.	6/9/18	-	Both 1st & relieved by troops of NEW ZEALAND Division and moved back to BACQUET RT and there billeted for PYS. The Bill-Bn ("A" & B) being in camp at about 12 NOON. Refit and cleaning up.	P.Y.4.
- " -	7.8.9-10.4.15	-	This period was spent in training and reorganisation, the following points being given special attention. Musketry including rapid fire and range practices P.T. & B.F. Close order drill, Saluting drill. Nightly Patrols using visual Signal communication and Company Schemes in co-operation with M.Gs and L.T.Ms.	P.Y.4.
- " -	21/9/18.	-	Bombing and Lewis Gun Classes were formed and Stretcher Bearers were given instruction by M.O. Lectures to Officers and NCOs were given in the afternoon on various subject included "Hints" reports and conveying information "Map Reading" rice. Demonstrating of Infantry working in co-operation with Tanks were witnessed. Recreational training included - Football Matches Boxing & Rifle Competition. This was devoted to Bathing and the disinfecting of clothing.	P.Y.4.
LF BVC QUARRE 22/9/18	-	-	Brigade moved up into Divisional Reserve. The Battn took over camp at I.29c from 7th MIDDLESEX REGT.	P.Y.4.
- " -	23/9/18	-	Cleaning up of Battle and camp area. Commanding Officers inspect. Athletic Class Order drill and musketry carried out in morning. Information respecting attack. Preliminary reconnaissance by C.O. + O.C. Co's for proposed attack.	P.Y.4.
- " -	24/9/18	-	Baths and training. Reachil King in afternoon. Practice attack to trench attack.	P.Y.4.

WAR DIARY

INTELLIGENCE SUMMARY

(Erase heading not required.)

Sheet 4.
1/8 LANCASHIRE FUSILIERS

Army Form C. 2118.

Place	Date	Hour	Summary of Events and Information	Remarks and references to Appendices
Ky Map Ref 57d 1/40000	25/9/18	—	Training - PT & BF. Rapid loading. Chev order drill. Attack practice. Battle.	SM4
LEBOCQUIERE			Further Brigade Conference. Attack arrangements made to perfect Scheme. Informed of Tank co-operation for 1st & 2nd Objective. Further reconnaissance by C.O. and O.C. Coys during the afternoon. Assembly positions in Q.5.A and C. and Q.9.B. reconnoitered. Move by motor bus Subject to take place at noon 26th inst.	
—	26/9/18	—	O.C. conference & O'Company Commanders re operations. Operation order D/28/9/18. Objectives:- 1st Objective From Q.5.A. 10.5 along CHAPEL WOOD SWITCH, DERBY & STAFFORD TRENCHES to Q.5.D. 60.25. 2nd Objective BROWN LINE along road from Q.6.B. 55.50 to Q.6.D. 25. 30. 3rd Objective YELLOW LINE from R.1.B. 05. 50 to R.1.D. 05. 60. 4th Objective BLUE LINE HIGHLAND RIDGE from R.2.A. 50.50 to R.2.B. 20.70. Battn ready to move at 1 p.m. Entrained at 6 p.m. and rested forward from RUYAULCOURT at 7.30 p.m. Moved to Assembly positions. Battn HQr's established at Q.10.B. 80.10.	SM4
TRESCAULT	27/9/18	—	Battalion in Assembly position by 2 A.M. The Battn attacked at 5.2 A.M. and found that the barrage did not fall on enemy Objective. Heavy casualties incurred through enemy machine gun fire from front and both flanks. All Officers of 'C' Company killed or wounded and only N.S. Officer of 'A' Company remained. Casualties up to 8.15 A.M. 5 Officers 132 O.R's — mostly attributed to M.G. fire from guns not affected by our barrage. Certain men of the 2nd Wave reached 1st Objective capturing many Prisoners and M.G's and again pushed forward 2 p.m. 6 p.m. SONIKEN ROAD Q.6. RVC held and patrols out forward	SM4
		12 noon 6.15 p.m.	1st Objective recaptured.	

Army Form C. 2118.

WAR DIARY
INTELLIGENCE SUMMARY

Sheet 5.

(Erase heading not required.) 1/8 LANCASHIRE FUSILIERS.

Place	Date	Hour	Summary of Events and Information	Remarks and references to Appendices
Ref Map Sheet 57c 1/40000 TRESCAULT	27/9/18	—	One platoon "A" Company reached BROWN LINE Q.6.B.7.D. At once afterwards ordered to withdraw to conform with Artillery barrage.	S4.
—	28/9/18	—	2:30 AM. Ond Company under barrage pushed to BROWN LINE. 1 PM. Two Companies leap frogged 8th LANCS FUSILIERS and made good general line established by 57m. along SONRAY ROAD running North through R.3.c + R.6.b. L/K tight patrols pushed forward to K.9. 3rd HKRLCW RIDGE. Touch was obtained and maintained on both flanks.	S4.
—	29/9/18	—	Division relieved by NEW ZEALAND Division. Battn. moved back to area Q.9.a.o.	S4. S4.
HAVRINCOURT WOOD	30/9/18	—	Battn. H.Qrs. situated Q.3.D.40.90. Day spent in cleaning up and reorganization.	S4.

James S. Hayfield
Lt. Col.
Commanding 1/8 Battn Lancs Fusiliers.

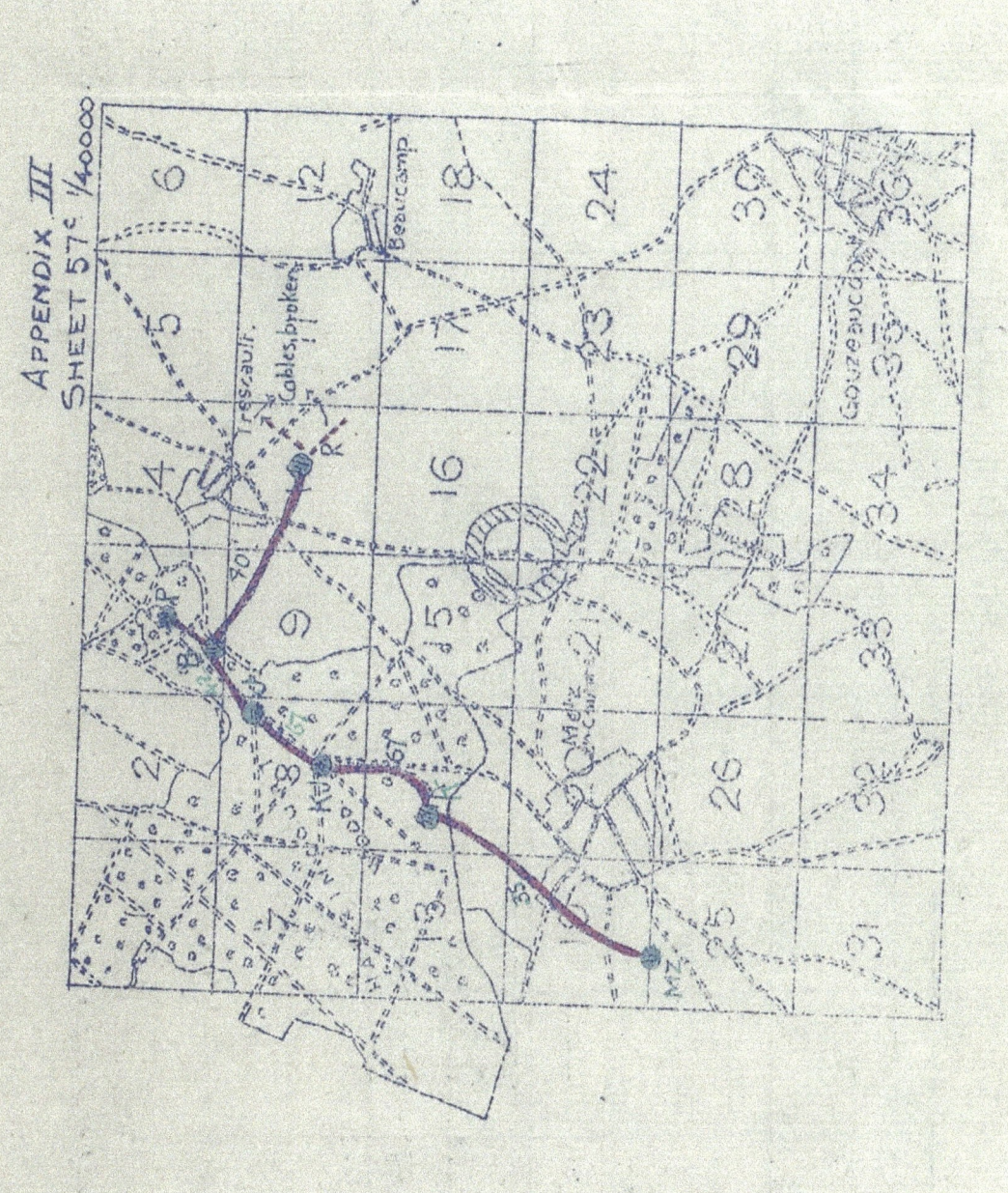

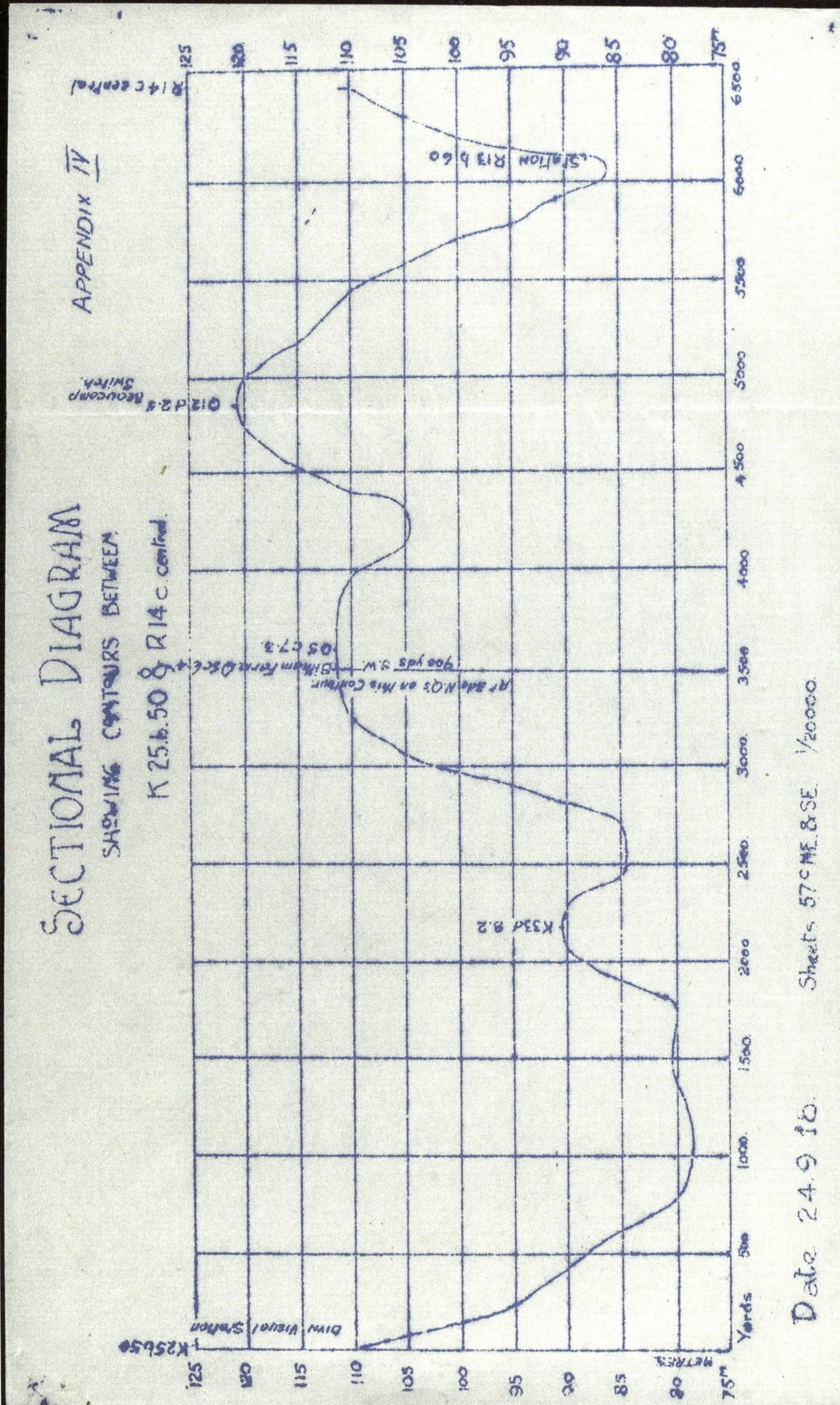

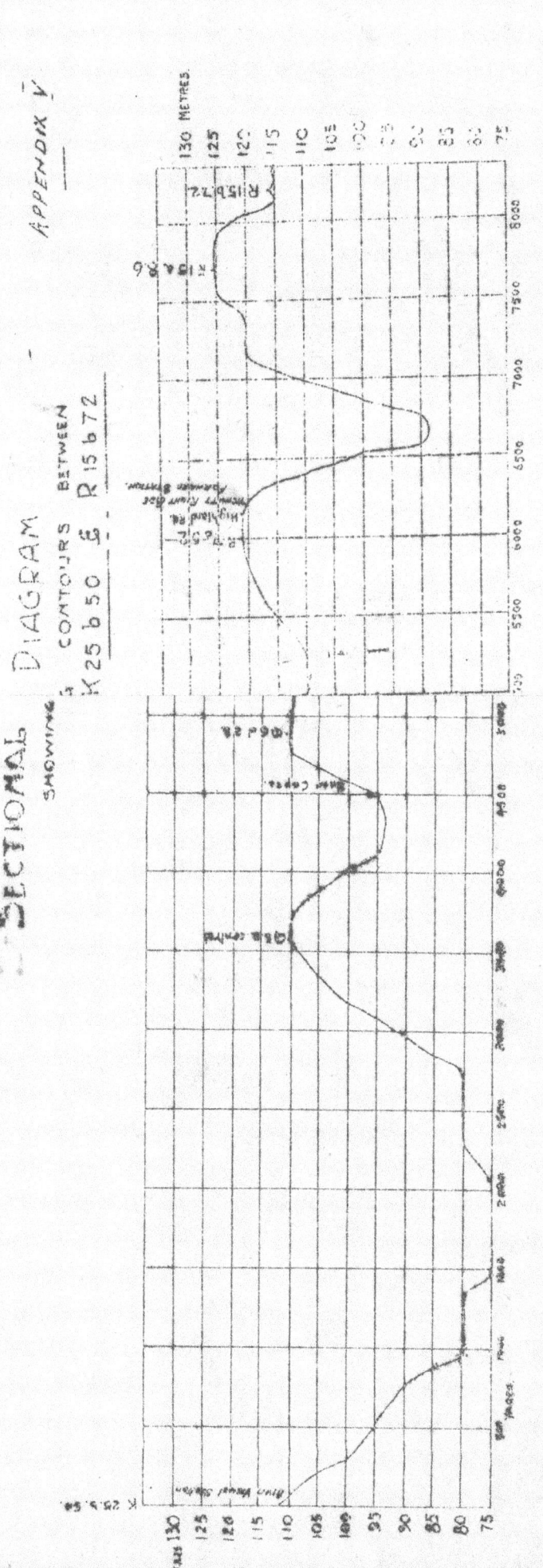

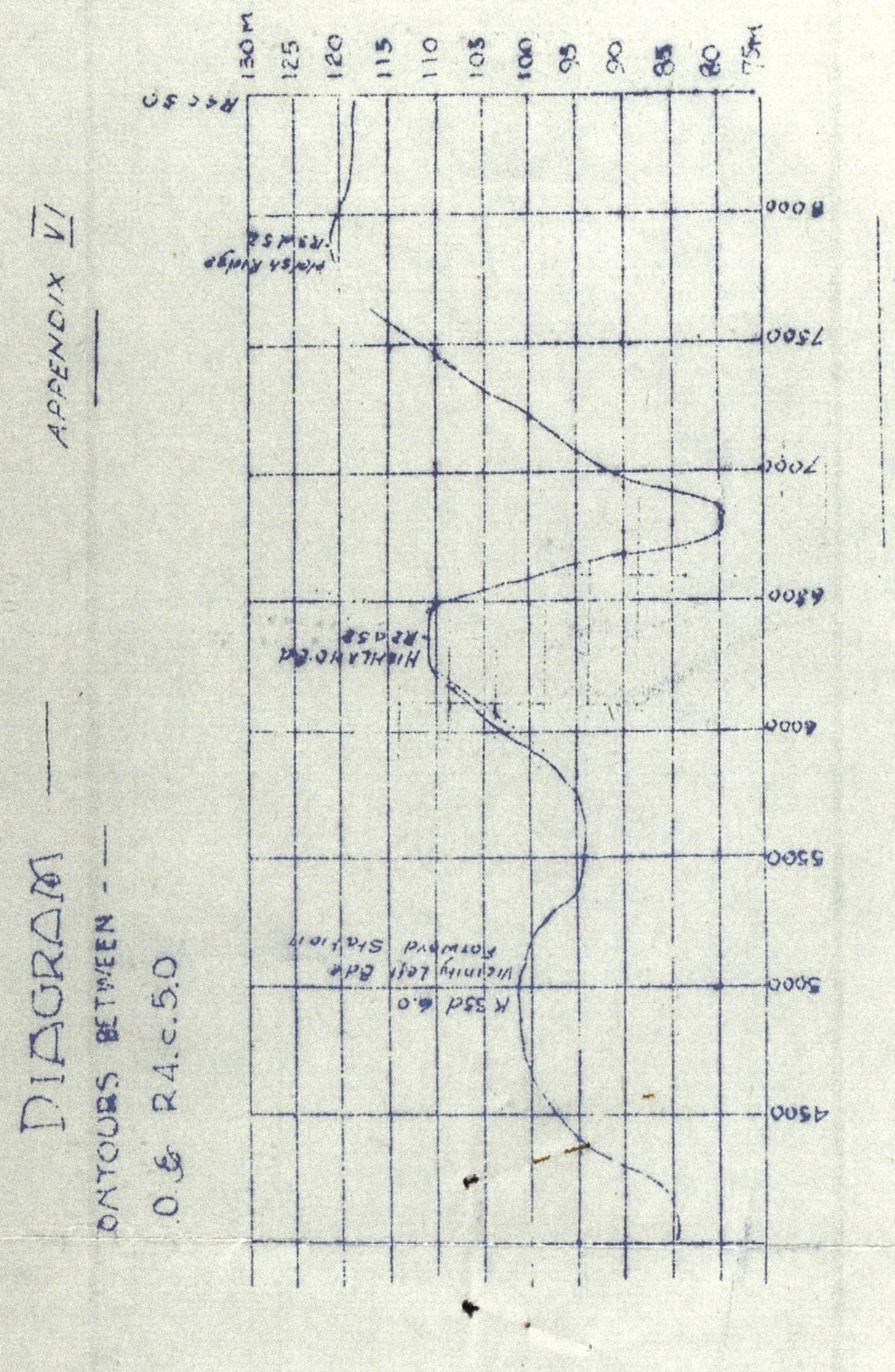

SECTIONAL
SHOWING C
K.25 65

K85050

130 METRES — Down Visual Station
125
120
115
110
105
100
95
90
85
80
75 M

Yards 500
1000 — Wigan Copse
1500
2000
2500
3000 — K35068 Vicinity proposed new N.C. Left B40 over road
3500
4000

Vol 21

H.O.N.
2H sheet

CONFIDENTIAL

WAR DIARY

of

1/8 LANCASHIRE FUSILIERS.

VOLUME 42.

From 1/10/18
To 31/10/18.

BON AVIS

VOL 42
Sheet 1.

Army Form C. 2118.

WAR DIARY
INTELLIGENCE SUMMARY

(Erase heading not required.) 1/8 LANCASHIRE FUSILIERS

Instructions regarding War Diaries and Intelligence Summaries are contained in F. S. Regs., Part II. and the Staff Manual respectively. Title pages will be prepared in manuscript.

Place	Date 1918	Hour	Summary of Events and Information	Remarks and references to Appendices
Ref Map sheet 57 C+11D20 7B HAVRINCOURT WOOD.	October 1st		During this period the Battn was in a bivouac Camp in HAVRINCOURT WOOD) carrying out reorganizing. Time was devoted to P.T, BFD, arm drill, musketry, rangt practice, tactical exercises, trench & French attack with tanks and live Lewis Machine gun & infiltration. Recreational training included football and sports.	S.U
- " -	8th		The Division being in Corps Reserve, were prepared to conform to advance. The Battn stood by ready for F at 07.00 A.M and then finally moved off putting into start point N.W. Sgt of TREFCOURT at 10.30A.M, and marche route to VILLERS PLOUICH Battn HQrs situated in R.13.B, Coys billeted in R.14.A+B by 13.15hrs.	O.O. 146 attached
VILLERS PLOUICH	9th		Battn moved off at 6A.M and marched via LA VACQUERIE – SONNET FARM – BONAVIS FARM – LE QUENNET – LES RUES-des-VIGNES to LE BOSQUET. Midday meals were served here and later further orders were received to move on via RATERIE – LESDAINS – de GRAND POINT to ESNES. Battn arrived and billeted in ESNES by 16.30hrs.	J.M.
ESNES.	10th		Lecture that afternoon by Brigadier General Cmdg on "Infiltration". Platoon demonstration arranged but cancelled owing to sudden orders to move. Battn marched via LONGSART	J.M

WAR DIARY Sheet 2

Army Form C. 2118.

1/8 LANCASHIRE FUSILIERS

Place	Date	Hour	Summary of Events and Information	Remarks and references to Appendices
Ry Map Sheet 57B 1/40000	1918 Oct 10th		To Road junction H.30.b. Hence by cross country tracks to Railway bridge in I.27.6. Billets here for the night.	JW
FONTAINE- AU-PIRE	11th	10.50	To FONTAINE-au-PIRE. Battn. marched via cross country tracks to HERPIGNY FARM D.25. Taking over accommodation vacated by N.Z. Division.	OO.118 attached JW
HERPIGNY FARM	12th		Morning spent in preparation for the line. At 16.30 hrs the Battn. moved off to relieve the 1st Battn. HERLINGTON REGT. Relief was held up owing to an attack by 12th HERLINGTONS at 18.00 hrs. Companies were dispersed in D.21.d. until this operation was over. The operation being completed the Battn. immediately moved up taking over the newly captured ground. Rain and intense darkness hampered all movement and added to the difficulties of the relief. Relief completed by 00.50 hrs. Battn. H.Qrs. situated D.28.A.50.10.	OO.119 attached
VIESLY + BRIASTRE	13th		Hostile shelling by trench mortars and support arms during the morning. Enemy counter attack in afternoon.	JW
— " —	14th		Visual contact in Cie. Orders received with regard to action to be taken in event of the enemy withdrawing. During the afternoon two posts were pushed forward up the slope towards BELLE VUE. One officer + other ranks led to sketches at Here.	See attached Appendix A.X/14 JW

WAR DIARY
INTELLIGENCE SUMMARY

1/8 LANCASHIRE FUSILIERS

Army Form C. 2118. Sheet 3.

(Erase heading not required.)

Place	Date	Hour	Summary of Events and Information	Remarks and references to Appendices
Ref. Map Sheet 57B 1/40000 NEUVILLE and BRIASTRE	12th October 14th		Has no co-operation with the troops on left and the post was hit heavily enfiladed by hostile MG fire.	App/.
- " -	15th		Relieved by 1/7 Batt. LANCASHIRE FUSILIERS and moved back to position vacated by them, becoming Batt. in Support. Relief complete without incident by 19.30 hrs.	O.O. 120 App/.
D.26.A.9.2.	16th 17th		Wet and dull weather. Days mainly spent in improving bivouacs. Remainder of day spent in improving bivouacs.	App/.
- " -	18th		Day spent in salving the Battle Area. Inspection and Baths. Neither 1/7 Lancashire nor 125th Inf Bde were relieved in the Line by 126th Inf Bde but the 1/8 LANCASHIRE FUSILIERS remained in position attached to the 126 Inf Bde as counter attack troops.	App/. App/.
- " -	19th		Inspection. Baths and Salvage.	App/.
- " -	20th		Heavy rain fell throughout the day. Called upon by 127 Bde to attack but orders were cancelled just as the Batt. was moving off. 125 Inf Bde in Divisional Reserve (in O.O.121)	App/.
- " -	21st		The Batt. relieved the 116th Manchester Regt in the Line, moving off from present position at 19.30 hrs and assembly for tea in E.19.A. Company Commanders conference was held here. Final instructions and all information obtainable of the new front were given. Relief was completed without incident by 23.00 hrs. Batt. HQrs situated at ERAS.	O.O. 122
E.14.a.5.1				App/.

WAR DIARY

INTELLIGENCE SUMMARY

Army Form C. 2118.

Sheet 4

1/8 LANCASHIRE FUSILIERS

Place	Date	Hour	Summary of Events and Information	Remarks and references to Appendices
By My Post 57 3 1/20500 S.E.of SOLESMES SUNKEN ROAD	19th Octr 21st		Dispositions of Companys after relief at night "A" Coy (R) 'B'Coy (L) in out-post line. Running from X Rds in E.2.b. S to K N.E. edge of MAROU. 'C'Cy (R) "D" Cy (L) in support to	
K.14.A.5.1.		1/50	front Cos situated in K.2.d. and K.9.a. on Eastern edge of BEANS BROOK	YM.
	22nd		Received orders regarding the attack to take place tomorrow. Conference of Coy Commanders and Staff. Orders issued — front line battalion consist of "A"Cy, "B"Cy, + "D"Cy.	See O.O. 123 attached
			'D'Cy detailed for special jot and bPaths in rear of "B"Coy. forward dept centr. fixed at E.3.b.9.5.	YM.
	23rd	—	Battn attached according to plan and carried all objectives	See A/x+ attached
			At 08.90 hrs the NEW ZEALAND Division passed through and continued the advance. The Battn remained in position until 12.30 hrs when in accordance with orders this Bn. withdrew and marched to billets in VIESLY	Order NO 174 24
VIESLY	24th	—	Moved at 12.00 hrs to billets in FONTAINE-au-PIRE. Battn in billets by 19.60 hrs.	Order no 125 24
FONTAINE au-PIRE	25th	—	Days spent in re-organization, re-equipping, bathing, cleaning of billets and clearing up generally. Adjutant and one officer pr Coy reconnoitered training areas.	YM.

Army Form C. 2118.

WAR DIARY Sheet 5.
INTELLIGENCE SUMMARY.
(Erase heading not required.)

1/8 LANCASHIRE FUSILIERS

Place	Date	Hour	Summary of Events and Information	Remarks and references to Appendices
Ref Map Sheet 19.8 5/3 1/40000 FONTAINE-AU-PIRE.	Sept 1918 27	—	Church parade.	M.M.
	28		Battn. Training in area I.21. Battn. parade in morn'g – physical train'g, salut'g, drill, Musketry, sit range practice. Demonstration in fire and movement at 148 A' grd. and crew. NCO's class. L.G. classes for instructors and recruits. Signalling Scouts & Snipers – Special tuition. Recreational train'g in afternoon.	
				M.M.
	30.		C.O's Parade. Individual train'g. Range practice. R.T. & R.T. Gas drill and schet'g. Platoon scheme by '1' platoon J.F.Coy. Boxing competition in afternoon.	M.M.
	31st		Rain hampered out-door train'g. Individual classes continued in billets. Lectures by Officers to N.CO's + Men. Recreational train'g and talks in after—	M.M.

James S. MacLeod
Lt Col
Commandy 1/8 Lancashire Fusiliers.

Illegible.

SECRET.

1/8th. LANCASHIRE FUSILIERS.

OPERATION ORDER NO 112.

11/10/18.

Reference 57 B 1/40,000

1. 1/8th. Lancashire Fusiliers will move today by march route to area J 1 and D 25.

2. DETAILS OF MARCH.

   Starting Point   J.15.d.2.6.
   Route.   Cross-Country tracks.
   Order of march. "A", "B", "C", "D" Coys. Battn H. Qrs.
   Head of column to pass starting point at 10. 35.
   200 yards interval will be maintained between Coys.
   First Line transport will follow in rear of Battn.

3. Strict march discipline will be observed.

4. Falling out states and location reports to be rendered to Battn H. Qrs on arrival.

5. Cookers will report to Transport Lines by 10. 15 this morning.

6. Officers' mess stores to be packed on Lewis Gun limbers.

7. A C K N O W L E D G E.

Lieut.
A/Adjt. 1/8th. Lancashire Fusiliers.

DISTRIBUTION AS PER O.O. 117.

COPY NO. 10

1/8th. LANCASHIRE FUSILIERS.
OPERATION ORDER NO 112.

Ref: Map sheet 57B N.E. 1/20.000   Field 12/10/18.

1. The 1/8th Bn Lancashire Fusiliers will relieve the 1st Battn
   Wellington Regt in the Right Sub-Sector of the Divisional Front
   tonight 12/13th October.

2. "A" Coy will relieve the 17th RUAHINE Coy   (Right Front.)
   "B" "   "   "   "   9th HAWKES BAY Coy (Left Front)
   "C" "   "   "   "   11th TARANKI Coy   (Support)
   "D" "   "   "   "   7th WELLINGTON W.C COY (Reserve)
   BATTN H. Qrs is situated at - D.26.c.50.10.

3. DETAILS OF MARCH.   The Battalion will march off from its present
   positions in the following order :-
                     "D" "A" "B" "C" Coys.   Bn H. Qrs.
   "D" Company will move off at 16.30.
   STARTING POINT. Road Junction D.25.c.50.20.
   ROUTE.   VIESLEY Rd to X Roads D.26.c.90.60. thence North along
   Valley, following line of 125 Contour to Area G.21.d.
   All movements East of road GAUDRY - QUISEY to be in Artillery
   formation.
   DRESS.   Fighting Order. Rations for 13th inst to be carried
   on the man.

4. Guides will be met ~~on railway~~ ~~at~~ D.21.d central at 1700.

5. Battn Forward report centre will be established at GALATAS.

6. Orders re Lewis Gun limbers will be issued later.

7. Rear H. Qrs. Q.M. Stores and Transport Lines will move to D.26.d.

8. Certificates stating that present billets have been left in a clean
   and sanitary condition will be rendered to the Orderly Room by 1600.

9. Completion of relief will be notified to Battn H. Qrs By code
   word "HASTER and DEAR".

10. A C K N O W L E D G E.

                                                    D W Johnson
                                                           Lieut.
                                          A/Adjt. 1/8th Lancashire Fusiliers.

Issued at .... p.m.
Copies to :-
1.   C.O.
2.   War Diary.
3/6. O. C. Companies.
7.   Quartermaster.
8.   Transport Officer.
9.   H. Q. Coy.
10. 1st Battn Wellington Regt.
11. File.

A.x/1.

Head Quarters
125 Infantry Bde.
~~~~~~~~~~~~~~~

Herewith short summary of operations of today 18th inst:—

4 pm. Intermittent shelling of support company front BRIASTRE and VIESLY

4.12 pm A very heavy barrage was put down on our front line, BRIASTRE and VIESLY.

4.30 pm Commanding Officer reported to Bde and our barrage was opened on S.O.S. lines.

5 pm Intelligence Officer reported that Infantry movement was seen on right flank but none opposite Battn. front.

5.15 pm Officer commanding forward Coys reported heavy attack and right front posts of Battn driven in. Left Coy front holding good. Casualties heavy.

2.

5.15pm Two platoons sent forward to re-inforce.

5.20pm Intelligence Officer sent forward to ascertain situation and report.

5.30pm Officer commanding forward companies confirmed 5.15pm information and reported stating that he was going forward to ascertain situation.

5.40pm Situation unchanged. By this time all available men at Coy HQrs had been pushed forward by orders of Capt H.D. Cumming MC. to re-establish right flank of Batt.
Not in touch with Division on Right.
Again confirmed information that left front coy was holding its original position.

6pm O.C. front line companies reported that all available men had been sent forward to re-establish situation around BELLE VUE and if necessary to form a defensive flank to the South

6 pm. Situation in COPSE E.19.A.4.4 acute. Casualties heavy. Wounded men report line withdrawn from BELLE VUE

6.15 pm. Situation explained to Brigade.

6.30 pm. Information received – Right flank Coy strength 27, Left flank Coy strength 50.

7 pm. Line now runs along road East of river in D.24 b and d. Heavy artillery and M.G. fire directed on forward areas.

7.30 pm. Patrols sent forward to find out situation and keep touch with enemy. Heavy M.G. fire encountered.

9 pm. Patrols report enemy M.G. posts at E.19.C.4.7, E.19.A.4.3 and E.19.C.2.6.
Reliable communication established with Division on Right.
Liaison post established at D.24.D.75.30.

9

The situation is now quiet with intermittent shelling of BRIASTRE and forward areas.

Enemy M.G. posts are being harassed by L.T.Ms and Field artillery during night.

A patrol has been pushed out on Left flank to get in touch with MOZA.

Casualties are roughly estimated as follows:-

1 Officer Killed 2 Officers Wounded
50 O.R. Killed and Wounded.

Lt Col
Commanding MOHU.

02.38
14/10/18

Rear OR
War Diary
May

SECRET.   COPY NO. 2

1/8TH LANCASHIRE FUSILIERS.
OPERATION ORDERS NO 120

REF MAP SHEET 57b N.E. 1/20,000   FIELD 15/10/18.

1. Warning Order No A.2. is confirmed.
   The 1/8th Lancashire Fusiliers will be relieved by the 1/7th
   Lancashire Fusiliers tonight 15/16th October 1918.

   "A" Coy MOHU will be relieved by "A" Coy MOWE.
   "B"   "   "   "   "   "   " "B" "   "
   "C"   "   "   "   "   "   " "C" "   "
   "D"   "   "   "   "   "   " "D" "   "

   On completion of relief the Battalion will move back to areas
   vacated by 1/7th Lancs Fus being disposed as follows :-

   Battalion H.Q.   D.26.a.8.2.
   "A" Company   D.22.c.
   "B"   "   D.21.a.
   "C"   "   D.20.c.
   "D"   "   D.26.a.

2. Companies will arrange to send advance parties to take over their
   new areas.

3. Rations and water will be delivered to your new Company H.Q. tonight.

4. Ammunition, bombs, picks and shovels will be handed and taken
   over and receipts obtained. Copies of receipts obtained will be
   handed in to Battn Orderly Room by 1800.

5. Guides as under will be sent to be at Battn H.Q. by 5. p.m.

        1   for each Company H.Q.
        1   for each platoon (MOWE has only two platoons per Coy)

6. Petrol tins will not be handed over but will be carried out by
   Companies.

7. Disposition sketches showing Company dispositions in new area will
   be rendered to reach Battn H.Q. by 0.900 16th inst.

8.9 ACKNOWLEDGE.

                                         [signature]
                                              Lieut.
                                         A/ADjt, MOHU.

Issued at.
Copies to 1 to C.O.
          2.   W.D.
          3.   O.C. "A" Coy   8. Completion of relief to be notified
          4.   O.C. "B" "   to Battn H.Q. by code word "BERNIER".
          5.   O.C. "D" "
          6.   O.C. "D" "
          7.   Signal Officer
          8.   Q.M. & T.O
          9.   Rear H.Q.
         10.   File.

SECRET   COPY NO.

1/8TH LANCASHIRE FUSILIERS
OPERATION ORDERS NO 121.

REF MAP SHEETS
57.S.E.E.)
51.a.S.E.) 1/20,000
57.b.   1/40,000.   FIELD OCT 19TH 1918.

---

1. The Third Army is resuming the advance on the 20th October. ZERO Hour will be at 0200 hours.

2. Trace showing boundaries and objectives of attack of :-
    (a) 42nd Division.
    (b) Flanking Divisions.
   will be forwarded later to ~~Units of 126th Inf Bde Group~~ only. O.C. C/8

3. The 5th Division is attacking on the right of the 42nd Division and the 62nd Division on the Left.

4. The attack on the 42nd Divisional Front will be carried out in two phases :-

   PHASE 'A' By 126th Inf Group, who are advancing to the GREEN LINE.

   PHASE 'B' By 127th Inf. Bde Group, who are leap frogging the 126th Inf Bde Group in the GREEN LINE, and advancing to the BROWN LINE.

5. The attack of the Division is being supported by six Brigades of Field Artillery, one Brigade Heavy Artillery, M.T.M's and L.T.M's.

6. The 125th Inf. Bde Group is in Divisional Reserve and by 1900 hours tonight will be disposed as follows:-

125th Inf. Bde Group H.Qrs.	AULICOURT FARM Area.
1/5th Lancashire Fusiliers.	In present positions.
1/7th Lancashire Fusiliers.	AULICOURT FARM.
1/8th Lancashire Fusiliers.	HEPIGNY FARM Area.

7. If necessary the N.Z Division is prepared to pass through the 42nd Division on the night 20th/21st October and continue operations on the 21st October.

8. The strictest measure must be taken to maintain secrecy.

9. Watches will be synchronised by Battalion Signal Officer at 2200 hours

10. <u>Distinguishing Badges.</u>
    The 15th Inf. Bde, 5th Division will wear a white tape over the Left shoulder under the right arm.
    The 95th Inf. Bde will wear a white tape tied on to the left shoulder strap.
    The 62nd Division will wear a white band on the left arm.

11. The watchword for 42nd Division will be "WON BETTER".

12. ACKNOWLEDGE.

                                               [signature]
                                                    Lieut.
                                     A/Adjt, 1/8th Lancashire Fusiliers.

P.T.O.

Issued at..............

Copies to:-

1. C.O.
2. War Diary.
3. O.C."A" Coy.
4. O.C."B" Coy.
5. O.C."C" Coy
6. O.C."D" Coy.
7. Q.M. & T.O.
8. O.C.Headquarters.
9. Intelligence Officer
10. Spare.

SECRET   COPY NO 2

1/8TH LANCASHIRE FUSILIERS
OPERATION ORDER NO 122

REF 57.b.N.E. 1/20,000   FIELD 21.10.18.

---

1. The Battalion will move up to relieve 1/6th Battn. MANCHESTER Regt this afternoon.

2. Details of march.

   Starting point: CROSS ROADS D.16.c.4.5.
   Route.   Direct to starting point thence East to
                  STATION BRIASTRE through village to assembly
                  positions E.13.c. where tea will be served.
   Order of March. "B", "A", "C" "D" Companies, Battalion H.Q.
   Head of Column to pass starting point at 1430 hours.

3. Transport Officer will arrange for cookers to proceed to Assembly positions.

4. Mess cart and 1 limber to report to Battalion Headquarters forthwith.

5. Company Commanders meeting upon arrival at E.13.c.

6. ACKNOWLEDGE.

                                                    Lieut.
                                A/Adjt, 1/8th Lancashire Fusiliers.

Issued at 1300 hours.

Copies to.
    1   to C.O.
    2/3 War Diary
    4/7 O.C.Companies
    8   Q.M.
    9. T.O.
    10. File.

Telegram.

MONU.

A.11.   21.

Order No 122. A Echelon transport including Lewis Gun Limbers tool limbers S.A.A. limbers water carts and pack animals will proceed on receipt of this order to D.24.b. on E side of LA SELLE RIVER AAA B Echelon and Rear H.Q. will move to D.28.a. applying to Town Major VIESLY for accommodation.

JUNE.

C.O.   O i/c Rear H.Q.
H.Q. Company   R.S.M.
Companys
Q.M.
T.O.
M.O.

SECRET.   COPY NO
                  1/8th LANCASHIRE FUSILIERS ORDER NO 128
                                                              22/10/18.
Ref 57b N.E.)
    51a. S.E.) 1/20,000
    A special map issued to ~~those~~ all recipients

1. The advance will be resumed by Third Army on 23rd inst.
    Fourth and First Armies will co-operate.
    ZERO hour will be 0200, at which hour the V Corps will attack.

2.(a) The boundaries and objectives of attack of the 42nd Div are
      shown on the map already issued.
  (b) The 5th Div is attacking on the right of the 42nd Div, and the
      3rd Div on the Left.

3.(a) The 125th Inf. Bde will carry out the attack being made by the
      42nd Div.
  (b) On conclusion of this attack the 2nd N.Z.Bde will go through the
      125th Inf Bde and continue the advance.

4.(a) The Bde will attack with the 7th Lan Fus on the right, and the
      8th Lan Fus on the Left, and the 5th Lancs Fus in support.
  (b) The inter Battalion boundary will be B.5.d.0.2 - E.4.b.0.6.-
      W.23.d.3.0.
  (c) The attack will be made in four bounds viz :- to the GREEN dotted
      line, the RED dotted line, the BROWN dotted line, and BLUE line.
      (Final Objective of Bde).
  (d) 1/8th Lan Fus are attacking with three companies advancing to
      furthest objective. In addition one platoon is being detailed
      on map to each of the following areas:-
      (1) Cross roads W.27.d.9.5. and COPSE W.27.d.
      (2) Railway in W.22.a and W.28.b. as shown in ringed points
          in special map.
  (e) The 5th/Lan Fus will support the attack of the Right Battn with
      two companies and the attack of the Left Battn with two Companies.
      These Companies will be under orders of Right and Left Battn
      Commanders without reference to Brigade H. L.
      In the normal event 1 Company supporting Right Battn will move to
      GREEN dotted line, 1 to BROWN line in Right Battn area. Similarly
      the two Companies supporting Left Battn will move to BROWN line
      in that Battn area.
      Companies of 5th Lancs Fus will be prepared to assist attack or
      to form defensive flanks or otherwise mop up, hold tactical points
      as required
  (f) Time table of attack has been issued separately.
  (g) The 1/8th Lancs Fus will attack with "A" Company on the Right,
      "B" Company centre and "C" Company on the left, "D" Company
      providing two platoons to mop up the areas mentioned in above
      sub para (d). Inter Coy boundaries as per map already
      issued.

5. Companies will form up along road in E.5.d and E.3.b. Forming up will be complete by 0130 hours. Assembly complete reports will be wired to Battn H.Q. using Surname of Company Commander as code word.

6. 22 Machine Guns of "C" and "D" Companies 62nd M.G.Battn are available for purposes of consolidation of the BLUE line and also for covering the advance of the 2nd N.Z. Inf. Bde when it goes through.

7. 125th L.T.M.B. will arrange for 6 guns to fire during initial barrage as follows:-
    (a) 2 Guns from positions in E.9.b. to fire on targets in E.10.a.
    (b) 4 Guns from positions in E.5.b. and E.5.d. to fire on Cross roads in E.4.b.
    After initial barrage Guns as in (a) come under orders of O.C. 1/7th Lancs Fus. Guns as in (b) under orders O.C. 1/8th Lancs Fus. for use during the advance and for consolidation.

8. (a) 2 Brigades of Field Artillery together with 62nd Div M.T.M. Batteries will support the attack of the Brigade.
    (b) The barrage will fall at ZERO plus 60 on the initial line E.10.a.0.7. - E.9.d.7.7. - E.4.a.4.5. - E.27.d.65.45.
    (c) The creeping barrage will advance at the uniform rate of 100 yards in 6 minutes, on the flanks, but will be slower in the centre, to the protective line of the BLUE objective.
    (d) Smoke shell will be fired to indicate the arrival of the barrage on the BLUE protective line. Smoke shells will also be fired to screen the troops on the BLUE line after daylight until the N.Z. Division has passed through.
    (e) At 0635 a barrage will be put down 200 yards East of BLUE LINE. At 0640 this barrage will lift and the 2nd N.Z. Inf. Bde will pass through the 125th Inf. Bde and continue the advance.

9. Direction during the advance will be kept by the following means:-
    (a) Compass Bearing. All Officers will have Compass Bearings of their objective. Compass Bearing of Advance is 90 Degrees Mag.
    (b) Thermites will be fired along both Divisional Boundaries, 800 yards in front of the advancing infantry. A Thermiut Beacon will also be fired by 1 Gun on E.4.b.3.6. to give general direction of inter-battalion boundary. This Beacon will be fired on a point 800 yards further East, when infantry get within 600 yards of E.4.b.3.6.
    It will be necessary to pay the greatest attention to direction owing to the fact that the barrage is falling in Echelon to the line of advance.

10. Handshakes with flanking Divisions will be as follows:-

NORTHERN DIVISION.
(a) Corner of Wood N.27.a.5.5.
(b) Road N.27.d.9.8.
(c) Railway N.28.a.4.6.
(d) Junction of Road and Railway N.28.b.2.9.

11. SIGNAL ARRANGEMENTS. Communications will be maintained to the Advance Report Centre by runner and Visual and from the Advance Report Centre to Batn H.q. by telephone, runner, visual and pigeon.

12. Contact aeroplane will call for flares at 0700 hours.

13. A Bde representative will visit units of Bde Group to synchronise watches before 2200 hours tonight.

14. Batt H.Q. will remain at L.14.a.8.6.. An Advance Report Centre will be established at Cross Roads H.8.b. at 2120 hour

15. An Advance Aid Post will be established at 0200 hours at L.9.c.4.7..
Stragglers post and Prisoners of War collecting station will be established at 0130 hours at Cross Roads H.14.b.

16. A Batt representative will visit Companies to synchronise watches before 2400 hours tonight.

17. ACKNOWLEDGE.

Wm. Fairhurst
Captain.
Adjutant 1/8th Lancs Fus.

Issued at.
Copies to
1 C.O.
2 O.C.,"A" Coy
3 O.C.,"B" "
4 O.C.,"C" "
5 O.C.,"D" "
6 O.C. H.Q.
7 War Diary
8 File.

W.D.

MEMO.

Order No 124. AAA. Companies will withdraw from present positions to billets in VIMY on receipt of this order AAA Any enemy left W of BLUE line will be dealt with vigorously by Companies before withdrawing. Transport for Lewis Guns etc will be at CROSS ROADS in B.14.c. AAA. Companies will move independantly AAA Route BELLE VUE - BRIASTRE - VIMY AAA Billet guides will meet at B.29.a.4.0. AAA Companies will report arrival in billets to Batt H.Q at the MAIRE AAA ACKNOWLEDGE.

                                                  Captain.
                                            Adjt, MEMO.

Copies to O.C. Companies
        Rear H.Q.
        Medical Officer
        R.S.M.

28/10/18.

Rec'd 1220

SECRET.   COPY NO. 12

1/8th. LANCASHIRE FUSILIERS ORDER NO 125.   23/10/18.

Refs 57B 1/40.000

1. 1/8th. Lancashire Fusiliers will move from VIESLY to BEAUVOIS tomorrow 24th inst.

2. Personnel will move by cross country tracks, transport by PRAYELLE – BETHENCOURT Road.

3. Starting Point   –   D.28.c.2.8.

4. Hour of March.   –   1200 hours.

5. Order of March   –   Battn H.Q.
   "A" Coy.
   "B" "
   "C" "
   "D" "
   Transport.

   Transport with transport personnel will move independently under orders of Transport Officer.

6. Arrival in billets will be reported to Battn H.Q.

7. Advanced billetting parties will report to Assistant Adjutant at Battn H.Q. at 0900 24th inst.   Guides will be detailed from these parties to meet Companies on arrival in BEAUVOIS.

8. All baggage will be stacked at Quartermaster's Stores by 1030 hours.

9. Battn H.Qrs will close at VIESLY at 1130 hours and reopen at BEAUVOIS on arrival.

10. A C K N O W L E D G E.

                                                              Capt.
                                    Adjt. 1/8th. Lancashire Fusiliers.

Issued at 1930 hours.

Copies to.
No 1   C.O.
   2.   2 i/c
   3.   "A" Coy.
   4.   "B" "
   5.   "C" "
   6.   "D" "
   7.   Q.M.
   8.   T.O.
   9.   M.O.
   10.   Sigs
   11.   R.S.M.
   12 & 13 W.D.
   14.   File.

Headquarters
125th Inf Brigade.

Reference Z 53 dated 23/10/18. The following is a short account of the mornings Operations.

Ref Map Sheet
57d.N.E)
51a.S.E) 1/20,000.

At 0326 hours Wednesday 23rd October 1918 the 1/8th Lancashire Fusiliers in conjunction with troops on left and right attacked. The attack was assisted by a creeping barrage. The Objective of this Battalion was the line (running from North to South) W.22.d.1.3. - East of loop railway line to W.28.b.3.4. thence South to W.28.d.4.2.

The Battalion attacked on a three Company front, "B" Company on Left, "C" Company Centre, and "A" Company on Right. Each Company in one wave of two lines.

"D" Company advanced in rear of "B" Company with the special object of mopping up and holding:-
(i) WOOD and CROSS ROADS in W.27.c.
(ii) RAILWAY in W.28. a & b.

Owing to heavy hostile Artillery and M.G. fire considerable difficulty was experienced in reaching assembly positions. The whole area was drenched with gas.

At 0326 hours the assembly troops went forward. To begin with strong resistance was met on both flanks but all opposition was overcome and Enemy M.G. nests cleaned up.

The WOOD and CROSS ROADS in W.27.d. and the road running S.E. through W. 28.c. were made good by 0344 hours. Determined resistance was met with here, many enemy being killed.

Enemy Artillery fire was non-effective. Certain M.G nests held out but these were energetically dealt with and the attack pushed forward to the final objective with force and determination. The whole of one Enemy M.G. post were bayoneted. Two of our men died from bayonet wounds.

The final objective was captured and posts pushed forward by 0 442 hours. Touch was maintained with 1st Battn Gordon Highlanders throughout.

At 0510 touch was obtained with the 7th Lancs.Fus in the final objective.

At 0520 it was reported that an enemy M.G. was still firing from the road junction in E.4.b. This was immediately dealt with and silenced.

Communication to Batt H.Q. was found difficult - all lines forward of Battn H.Q. were broken by enemy barrage previous to the attack and owing to mist Visual Stations were unable to be instituted. Runners experienced great difficulty in finding direction owing to mist.

Sheet No 1   Contd.

Headquarters
125th Inf. Brigade. (contd)

The total number of enemy dead, prisoners and captured material during the operation is as follows:-

Prisoners.	1 Officer	80	O.R. (including wounded)
Enemy dead	2 Officers	78	O.R.
M.G's		37	
Light Field Gun		1	
T.M.		2	

Our Casualties were :-

Killed		7	O.R.
Wounded	2 Officers	47	O.R.
Missing		5	O.R.

James S. MacLeod
Lieut. Colonel.
Cmdg, 1/8th Lancashire Fusiliers.

24/10/18.

CONFIDENTIAL

WAR DIARY.
OF
1/8 LANCASHIRE FUSILIERS.

VOLUME 43.

From 1/11/18   To 30/11/18.

WAR DIARY

INTELLIGENCE SUMMARY

Army Form C. 2118.

Sheet 1.

1/8 LANCASHIRE FUSILIERS

Place	Date 1918	Hour	Summary of Events and Information	Remarks and references to Appendices
Ref Map Sheet 57B 1/40,000 FONTAINE-AU-PIRE	November 1st		Route march. Route - Folk roads I.15.d.1.4 - Folk roads I.33.c.6.8.15 Folk roads HAUCOURT I.31.a.1.4., thence North to H.24.d.6.4. A halt of 30 minutes was called here for instruction. All ranks (by companies) in Map Reading, Topographical features & Compass Reading. At 11.30 hrs march was resumed to X Roads CATTENIERES H.12.d. Route South East to FONTAINE. Battn arrived in billets at 12.45 hrs. Received training in afternoon.	N.Y.
-"-	Nov 2nd		Training and Baths. Rain in morning. Supplies trigger dumps 10.55 hrs received war state positions of more training at AURICOURT FARM(?). Junior N.C.O.s and L.G. Classes sent to Divisional Reception Camp. Further orders received from Bde Stating more to take place on 7th inst.	N.Y.
-"-	3rd		Brigade Arm Country Race - Battn H.Qrs. farm lane pit. Church Parade. Divisional Band Competition. Battn took 12th [illegible] for Brass Band Competition. Orders received re more training.	N.Y.
-"-	4th		Bright and warm: Battn marched via BETHENCOURT - VIEZELEY - BELLE VUE to SOLESMES. Battn left FONTAINE at 13.10 hrs and was in billets at SOLESMES at 17.10 hrs. Fine water.	N.Y. O.O. 126.
SOLESMES	5th		Moved to BEAUDIGNIES. Marched off at 09.34 hrs and arrived at -"- area at 14.00 hrs. Heavy rain throughout the day. Billets very poor. Today's march latter a very unpleasant one owing to roads being in fair condition and blocked with traffic of all kinds.	N.Y. O.O.127. N.Y.

WAR DIARY
INTELLIGENCE SUMMARY

Sheet 2.

1/8 LANCASHIRE FUSILIERS.

Army Form C. 2118.

Place	Date 1918	Hour	Summary of Events and Information	Remarks and references to Appendices
Ruyaulcourt 51A & 51K OD. BEAUDIGNIES R.32.b.d.	6th	Noon	Moved to HERBIGNIES being billeted at 08.30 and arriving in billets in new area at 11.30 hrs. Heavy rain throughout the day. Brigade became Bde in support at 18.00 hrs & the Battn was held in readiness to move off at 1 hour notice. Battn HQrs situated in Rue du Lion.	OO.129 & OO.129. OO.130. Y.Y.
HERBIGNIES M.29 & 30	7th		Battn ordered to move to OBIES and left start point at 12.10 hrs. The destination was changed to HARGNIES at 13.05 hrs and march continued. News was received from advance parties that HARGNIES was only just clear of the enemy and was being heavily shelled. The Brigade Column therefore, was halted on the FOREST DE MORMAL on the FORESTER'S HOUSE — HARGNIES ROAD. At 17.00 hrs orders were received to proceed to LA HAUTE RUE and the proposed billets. The march was continued immediately and, inspite of some difficulty, billets were found. The Battn Hd Transport was in billets by 22.30 hrs. The Transport were unable to accompany the Battn owing to mine craters in road — the standstill caused at X ROADS RUE at 03.40 hrs 8th inst.	Y.Y.
LA HAUTE RUE O.33.C.	8th		Brigade became Bde in Right Divisional Front, and ordered to continue the advance. The Battalion became Battn in support with the special task of providing ADVTMOUNT and Korean Piks. At 10.30 hrs the Battn took up position in RAMSAY — a patrol was pushed forward into HAUTMOUNT and discovered that the town had been evacuated by the enemy. Enemy machine gunners and snipers still remained in the western outskirts of the town but these were dealt with and posts were established by Adv B.G.S. at P.74.c.2.8. P.74.c.2.b. & P.30.a.5.5. The remainder of the town — ex'g B.G.S. being in support in P.23.b.	Initial orders only was issued & copies Y.Y.

WAR DIARY

INTELLIGENCE SUMMARY

Army Form C. 2118.
Sheet 3.

1/8 LANCASHIRE FUSILIERS.

Place	Date	Hour	Summary of Events and Information	Remarks and references to Appendices
Ref Map Sht 19/18 5† 1/40000 P.33.R.2.4.	Nov 1918 8th		At 23.00 hrs the posts held by OTR Coys were taken over by 7th Lancs Fusiliers. These Companies then formed a defensive flank running Eastward of the Northern outskirts of the Town.	Ref.
"	9th		The 62nd Division on our left flank advanced into Hautmont. A+B Coys were thereupon withdrawn & billetted in HAUTMONT at 08.00 hrs. Batt HQrs moved forward and opened at P.29.C.4.8. at 13.30 hrs — C+D Coys moved to P.29a into billets. Rear HQrs and Transport who had been at LA HAUTE RUE since the evening of 7th inst also moved up and joined the Batt. in billets in HAUTMONT at 17.00 hrs.	Ref.
HAUTMONT	10th/11th	09.30	Commanding Officers Parade & Inspection. 12.00 hrs C.O's inspection of billets. Days spent in resting and cleaning up. Kit inspection etc.	Ref.
"	12	09.30	C.O's parade. 12.00 hrs C.O's inspect. billets. Company training in morning, recreational training in afternoon.	Ref.
"	13		C.O's parade. Coy training and recreational training. Important billet.	Ref.
"	14		C.O's parade followed by Route March. Daily Lectures Company Commanders gave instruction in map reading to Platoon Commanders and NCO's. Inspection of L.G. and a/t equipment by L.G.O. Recreated training including football and Tug-of-War (inter-company) during afternoon. Batt. Rehearsal in GRAND PLACE for tomorrows presentation of Band.	Ref.
"	15			

WAR DIARY
INTELLIGENCE SUMMARY

1/8 LANCASHIRE FUSILIERS

Army Form C. 2118.

Sheet 9.

Place	Date	Hour	Summary of Events and Information	Remarks and references to Appendices
Afft. Flat S1. 1/9050 HAUTMONT	1918 Novr 16	-	Ceremonial parade for presentation of Captured German gun to the Mayor and Township of HAUTMONT. The Batln was represented by a composite company of 6 Officers and 80 O.Rs.	Ref.
"	17	-	The remainder of the Battn spent the morning on the Range at P.34.A.3.1. Recreational training in afternoon.	Ref.
"	18	-	Church Parade. Brigade Parade Service in GRAND PLACE at 10.30 hrs. A & C Coys on Range. C & D Coys training by Companies. Battn cross country run in afternoon.	Ref. Ref. Ref.
"	19	-	Battn route march – dress full marching order.	Ref.
"	20	-	Construction of a Battn Range in P.34.A. during the day, the whole Battalion battled. Lewis Gun Class assembled under Splr Timms - 2 men per Company attending.	Ref.
"	21	-	A & B Coys – Company training in morning. C & D Coys worked on Range. Lewis Gun and Signallers Classes continued. Recreational training in afternoon included inter-platoon Assault. Football Competition and Tug-of-War.	Ref.
"	22	-	The Battalion less "A" Coy carried out a route march in marching order. "A" Coy on Butts at Battn Range P.34.A. Inter-platoon Football competition in afternoon.	Ref.
"	23	-	Company training carried out by A & C & D Coys, "B" Coy fired practices 1 & 2 on Battn Range. Battn Rugby Football Team played 55 Manchesters. Result - 55 Manchesters 6 points 5 Manchesters 6 points.	Ref.
"	24	-	Church Parade.	Ref.
"	25	-	Battn Route March cancelled owing to rain. Heavy spell in feet and tost inspection of Equipment.	Ref.

WAR DIARY

Sheet 5

Army Form C. 2118.

INTELLIGENCE SUMMARY

(Erase heading not required.) 1/8 LANCASHIRE FUSILIERS.

Place	Date 1918	Hour	Summary of Events and Information	Remarks and references to Appendices
Ref Map Sheet 51 IFROW HAUTMONT	Novbr 26		Brigade route march - children excluded. Dress full marching order. Recreational Training in afternoon.	Order No 131 Sell.
- " -	27		Morning spent in Batty Drill. Batten. Inter-platoon Arms Football Competition in afternoon.	Sell.
- " -	28		C.O.'s parade in red pattern full marching order. All companies carried out a route march first. Less than 4 miles during the morning. Inter-platoon football competition in afternoon. Divisional Cross-Country Competition in Denain.	Sell.
- " -	29		Range practice during morning on Pattern Range P.3 & A. Received this Officers Shooting Competition in afternoon. Divisional Boxing Competition Semi-finals in Denain.	Sell.
- " -	30		Batten Route March. Marched past Saluting point at 09.45 hours and returned to billet by 12.30 hrs. During the period spent in HAUTMONT much time has been spent in reorganisation. Regimental institutes have been organised, a Batten Officers Mess, Warrant Officers Sergeants Mess, Mens Dining Room and a Recreation and Reading Room have been instituted. The billets for all ranks are good.	S.W. — Order No 132 Sell. Sell.

M.W. Mair Major
Commanding 1/8 Lancashire Fusiliers.

SECRET   COPY NO........ 2

1/8th. LANCASHIRE FUSILIERS
OPERATION ORDER NO 126.

3/11/18.

Ref Sheets 57b 57A and 51.

1. The advance is being resumed by Fourth, Third and First Armies on 4th November. French armies are also co-operating.

2. (a) The attack on the IV Corps front is being carried out by the 37th Division on the Right and the N.Z. Division on the left. Boundaries and objectives are given on map which will be shown to O. C. Companies
(b) As soon as the RED LINE has been made good, the advance is being vigorously pressed to line of the ST RELY – CHAUSSEE – PONT SUR– SAMERE – BAVAI ROAD.

3. The 5th and 42nd Divisions are to be prepared to pass through the 37th and N.Z. Divisions respectively and to continue the advance

4. The strictest measures will be taken to maintain secrecy.

5. Four men per platoon will carry hatchets and bill hooks for cutting gaps in hedges. These tools will be issued by Quartermaster at SOLESMES.

6. (a) 1/8th. Lancashire Fusiliers will move to SOLESMES on Nov 4th.
   (b) Starting Point   –   Battalion H.Q.
   (c) Hour of march.   –   1310.
   (d) Order of march. :–

   Battalion H.Q.
   "A" Company.
   "C"   "
   1st Line Transport and Baggage Wagons.
   (e) Route. – BETHENCOURT – VIESLY – BELLE VUE.

7. Battalion H.Qrs will close at FONTAINE –au– PIRE at 1300 hours and re–open at SOLESMES on arrival.

8. Watches will be synchronised under arrangements to be made by Signal Officer.

9. A C K N O W L E D G E.

                                                        Capt.
                                    Adjt. 1/8th. Lancashire Fusiliers.

Issued at... 1600 ...by orderly.

Copies to :–
No 1.   C.O.   No 8. Quartermaster.
   2.   War Diary.   9 Medical Officer.
   3.   "   "   10 Battn Signal Officer.
   4. & 5   O.C. "A" Coy.   11 Intelligence Officer.
   6 & 7   "   "C" "   12 Transport Officer.
                                      13 R.S.M.
                                      14 125th Inf Bde (for information)
                                      15 File.

SECRET.

Battalion will be prepared to move off at half an hours notice after 0900 tomorrow morning.
Baggage wagons, maltese cart, mess cart will report at Battn H.Qrs at 0900.   All kits will be stacked at Battn H.Qrs by 0900.

[signature] Capt.
4/11/18.   Adjt. 1/8th. Lancashire Fusiliers.

Issued as per O.O. 126 less one copy to 125th. Infl Bde.

SECRET.

1/8th. LANCASHIRE FUSILIERS.
OPERATION ORDER NO 127.

5/11/18.

Ref Sheets 51 A S.W. and 57B N.E. 1/20,000.

1. 1/8th. Lancashire Fusiliers will move today the 5th inst to BEAUDIGNIES or, if BEAUDIGNIES is occupied by 127th Inf. Brigade Group to the VERTIGNEUL – PONT – a – PIERRES Area.

2. (a) Starting Point. – Battn H.Qrs.
   (b) Order of march – Battn H.Qrs.
                        "A" Coy.
                        "C" Coy.
                        First line transport and
                        baggage wagons.
   (c) Hour of march. – 0834.

3. ROUTE. Cross Roads E.4.b. – VERTIGNEUL – thence Infantry will use track W.15.b.9.1. to W.18.b.4.2. Transport will move via cross roads W.23.d.9.9. thence by W.17.c.1.2.

4. BILLETING PARTIES. Billeting party consisting of 2/Lieut Ladmore mounted and 5 Battn H.Qr Runners on cycles will proceed at 0700 and report to the Staff Captain at Fork Roads R.32.d.1.8 BEAUDIGNIES at 0700 hours today.
   0830

5. Reveille today at 0600.
   Breakfast.   0700.
   Sick parade.   0730.
   All baggage will be stacked at Battn H.Qrs at 0730.
   Baggage wagons, maltese cart, mess cart, and horses for field kitchens will report at Battn H.Qrs by 0730.

6. Watches will be synchronised under arrangements to be made by the Signal Officer at 0800.

7. A C K N O W L E D G E.

                                          Capt.
                        Adjt. 1/8th. Lancashire Fusiliers.

Issued at 0110 by orderly.

Issued as per O.O. 126 less one copy to 125th. Inf Bde.

SECRET.

1/8th. LANCASHIRE FUSILIERS.
OPERATION ORDER NO 128.

6/11/18.

1. 1/8th. Lancashire Fusiliers will move to HERBIGNIES today the 6th inst.

2. Starting Point — Cross Roads R.33.a.65.30.
   Hour of march. 0834 hours.
   Order of march. — "C" Coy.
                     "A" "
                     Battn H.Qrs.
                     First line transport and baggage wagons.

3. ROUTE. Road skirting North of LE QUESNOY to R.24.c.4.9. — M.19.d.2.5. — cross roads M.15.c.0.4. to VILLEREAU.

4. BILLETING PARTIES. consisting of 2/Lieut. Ladmore and 2/Lieut Timms and 5 orderlies from Battn H.Qrs will report to Staff Captain at FREMEDULIN, HERBIGNIES M.29.a. central at 0830. today the 6th inst.

5. Reveille.   0600.
   Breakfast.   0630.
   Sick Parade.   0730.
   All baggage will be stacked at the Quartermaster's Stores by 0730.

6. Watches will be synchronised by the Signal Officer at 0800.

7. A C K N O W L E D G E.

                                        Capt.
                    Adjt. 1/8th. Lancashire Fusiliers.

Issued at 0130 by orderly.

Issued as per O.O. 127.

SECRET.

1/8th. LANCASHIRE FUSILIERS
OPERATION ORDER NO 129.

6/11/18

1. The Battalion will be prepared to move at one hours notice from 1600 hours today 6th inst to support the 126th. Inf Brigade in the Line.

2. Companies will stand to on Company Alarm Posts on receipt of the order and report to Battn H.Qrs when ready to move.

3. Rear Battn H.Qrs and Transport Lines will remain at HERBIGNIES for the present, in case of a move as detailed in para 1.

4. Administrative instructions are issued seperately.

5. A C K N O W L E D G E.

Capt.
Adjt. 1/8th. Lancashire Fusiliers.

Issued at...1930..hours by orderly.

Issued as per O.O. 128.

SECRET

1/8TH LANCASHIRE FUSILIERS
OPERATION ORDERS NO 130.
────────────────────────
7/11/18.

1. The Battalion will be prepared to move forward to support the 126th Inf. Brigade at 0545 hours to-day.

2. Order of march. Battalion H.Q, "A" Company, "C" Company. Only the four Lewis Gun limbers will accompany the Battalion. Hour of march 0545 hours.
   Reveille 0400
   Breakfast 0430.   Starting Point - X roads M.29.b

3. All baggage surplus to requirements for the line will be stacked at Company H.Q. The Quartermaster will arrange to collect to the Q.M. Stores.

4. Details remaining behind at Transport Lines will report to the Asst/Adjutant at Quartermasters Stores immediately the Battalion has marched off.

5. Further orders will be issued with regard to Rear Headquarters and the remainder of the Transport.

6. A C K N O W L E D G E.

Captain.
Adjt, 1/8th Lancashire Fusiliers.

7/11/18.

Issued as per Operations No 129.
Issued at... 0030

COPY NO. 5

1/8th. LANCASHIRE FUSILIERS ORDER NO 131.

Ref Sheet 51 1/40,000.   25/11/18.

1. 125th. Inf. Bde is parading for a route march on Tuesday 26th inst.

2. 1/8th. Lancashire Fusiliers will pass the starting point - Cross Roads P.30.b.4.3. at 0947 hours, following in rear of 1/7th. Lancashire Fusiliers.

3. ROUTE. - S.P. P.30.b.4.3. - LES GRAVETTES Q.20.a.8.7. - LOUVROIL - FAUBOURG - ST LAZARE - Q.9.central - Fork Roads Q.17.c.4.3. - FERRIERE Q.22.b.9.3. - Q.23.c.4.6. - T. Roads Q.29.c.2.6. - Cross Roads Q.26.a.3.3. - FORT D'HAUTMONT. Distance 8 miles.

4. 1st Line Transport complete will accompany the Battn.

5. DRESS. Full marching order. Steel helmets will be worn. Small box respirators will not be carried.

6. Parade states will be handed in to Adjt on C.O's parade.

7. The following intervals will be maintained :-
   Between Coys..................................10 yds.
   Between Unit and its transport................50 yds.
   Between each section of twelve vehicles.......50 yds.
   Between Units.................................50 yds.

8. Strictest attention will be paid to march discipline as per Fourth Army G.S. 122 "Notes on march discipline" issued to all Officers and Warrant Officers.

9. The column will halt at 10 minutes to each clock hour and resume the march at the hour.

—2—

O.O. 13 continued.

10. 1/1st E.L. Fld Ambulance will provide one horsed ambulance to proceed in rear of the column. This ambulance will be at FORT D'HAUTMONT at 1000 hours.

11. A C K N O W L E D G E.

                       [signature]   Capt.
       Adjt. 1/6th. Lancashire Fusiliers.

Issued at...1230....by Orderly.

Distribution.

1.   C.O.
2.   W.D.
3.   "
4.   O.C. "A" Coy.
5.   "   "B" "
6.   "   "C" "
7.   "   "D" "
8.   O.C. H.Q. details.
9.   . M.
10.   T.O.
11.   R.S.M.
12.   M.O.
13.   125th. Inf. Bde.
14.   File.

SECRET.   COPY NO. 2

1/8th. LANCASHIRE FUSILIERS ORDER NO 132.
                                                                29:11:18.

Reference sheet 51. 1/40.000.

1. 125th. Inf. Bde is parading for a route march tomorrow the 30th inst.

2. 1/8th. Lancs Fus. will pass the starting point (Fork roads P.35.a.9.4. at 0946 hours) marching in rear of the 7th Lancs Fus.

3. Order of march :-   H. Qrs.   "A", "B", "C", "D" Coys.
                       1st Line Transport.

4. ROUTE. Fork roads P.35.a.9.4. -FONTAINE V.11.d.1.4. - LIMONT FONTAINE V.17.d.5.2. - V.23.b.7.6. - V.24.a.4.1.- CHURCH ECLAIBES - W. 24.d.2.4. - X Roads W.15.d.3.0.- BEAUPORT W.14.d.8.9. - W.14.b.8.8. - W.8.d.4.3. - W.1.b.4.1. - Fork roads Q.31.b.9.3. - FORT D'HAUTMONT - to billets.   Distance 8 miles.

5. DRESS. Full marching order. Steel helmets will be worn.

6. The following intervals will be maintained :-
    Between Coys............................10 yds.
    Between Unit and its transport........50 yds.
    Between each section of 3 vehicles...50 yds.
    Between Units...........................50 yds.

7. The strictest attention will be paid to Fourth Army G.S. 128 "Notes on march discipline" issued to all Officers and Warrant Officers.

8. The column will halt at 10 minutes to each clock hour and resume the march at the hour.

                                                                P.T.O.

9. O.C. 1/1st. E.L. Fd A.mb. will detail one horsed ambulance to be at the starting point P.35.a.9.4. at 0945 hours. This ambulance will proceed in rear of the column.

10. O. C. Signals will send a watch to Bde H.Qrs at 0800 hours tomorrow to be synchronised. This watch will afterwards be sent round to recipients of this order before 0845 hours.

11. A C K N O W L E D G E.

                                           Capt.
                 Adjt. 1/8th. Lancashire Fusiliers.

Issued at......hours by Orderly.

Copies to. :-

1.   O.O.
2.   W. D.
3.
4.   O. C. "A" Coy.
5.   "   "B" "
6.   "   "C" "
7.   "   "D" "
8.   O. C. H.Q. details.
9.   Q. M.
10.   T. O.
11.   R. S. M.
12.   M. O.
13.   125th. Inf. Bde.
14.   File.

CONFIDENTIAL

WAR DIARY

OF

1/8 LANCASHIRE FUSILIERS

FROM 1/5/18 TO 31/5/18

VOLUME 44

Army Form C. 2118.

WAR DIARY
Sheet 1.

INTELLIGENCE SUMMARY. 1/8 LANCASHIRE FUSILIERS

(Erase heading not required.)

Instructions regarding War Diaries and Intelligence Summaries are contained in F. S. Regs., Part II. and the Staff Manual respectively. Title pages will be prepared in manuscript.

Place	Date	Hour	Summary of Events and Information	Remarks and references to Appendices
Ref Map Sheet 51 1/40 000 HAUTMONT	Dec 1	9-30	C.O's Parade. The Battalion marched to cross roads O.20.a. and lined the MAUBEUGE – AVESNES road, O.20.a. – O.20.c. on the occasion of His Majesty the King's visit to the Fourth Army Area. His Majesty walked along the road between the ranks of the Division.	MM.
"	2.	"	C.O's Parade and inspection. The Battalion less "C" Coy proceeded to Range to carry out firing practices. "C" Coy were employed in salvage party in the area allotted under Divisional Salvage scheme. Afternoon :- Final Battalion Inter-platoon Renovation competition.	MM.
"	3	"	C.O's Parade for "A","B","C" coys, these coy's afterwards carrying range practices. "D" Coy on Salvage. Afternoon recreational training.	MM.
"	4	"	The Battalion less "A" Coy on C.O's Parade, then proceeding to Range for firing. "A" Coy on Salvage scheme. Football match in afternoon against 125 T.M.B.	MM.
"	5	"	Batts allotted to D Coy. A Coy on salvage. B & C Coys on C.O's parade, afterwards carrying out range practices. Rater Rugby match in the afternoon.	MM.
"	6	"	C.O's Parade for the Battalion less "B" Coy", the Battalion then proceeding for a short route march. B Coy on salvage. Afternoon recreational training. Lecture by Padre, battalion to on "The Industrial Revolution."	MM.
"	7	10.15	The Battalion Paraded under the R.S.M., drill, belt & bayonet. C.O's inspection of billets and Regt. Institutes. Afternoon – Inter-coaches Football. Final Brigade Competition V 1/5 L.F.	MM.

A5834 Wt.W4973/M687 750,000 8/16 D.D.&L.Ltd. Forms/C.2118/13.

Army Form C. 2118.

WAR DIARY

INTELLIGENCE SUMMARY.
(Erase heading not required.)

Sheet 2.
1/8 LANCASHIRE FUSILIERS

Place	Date 1918	Hour	Summary of Events and Information	Remarks and references to Appendices
1/8 Lanc Fus¹ St Hoooo HAUTMONT	Dec 8	1020	Church Parade. Divine Service in large factory P23d. for 1/7th & 1/8 L.F.	MWH
"	9	0930	C.O's Parade, dress Skeleton order. A & B Coys marched to range & continued firing range practices. C & D Coys carried out P.T. + games and close order drill. C.O's inspection of all Transport and Employed men. Recreational Training in afternoon.	MWH
"	10	"	C.O's Parade, Skeleton order. A & B Coys on range. C & D Coys carried out training as per yesterdays programme. Afternoon A Coy V C Coy. Association Football.	MWH
"	11	"	Brigade Route March, distance 8 miles. Dress :– full marching order. For route see :– Owing to heavy rain on reaching road junction Q31d. battalion returned to billets by route Q31d. – Q31c. – FORT d'HAUTMONT. Afternoon Officers v Sgts Rugby match cancelled. Rain.	Order NO 133 (1) MWH
"	12	"	C.O's Parade, Skeleton order. Heavy rain, battalion carried out wet day programme. Lecture to men, cleaning of equipment etc. Inspection of New draft by 2IC. C.O. inspected new drafts in Batt Recreation Room.	MWH
"	13	"	Heavy rain, wet day programme carried out. Lectures to men on educational subjects.	MWH
"	14	"	Moved to MAUBEUGE en route for CHARLEROI. Battalion left billets at 1138 hours and marched through LOUVROIL, arriving at RUE PETRUS, MAUBEUGE at 1340 hours, where the battalion billeted for the night. BHQ. established at No 31. RUE PETRUS.	O.O. 134 MWH
MAUBEUGE (NAMUR 8) Hu oooo	15	"	Battalion continued route march, leaving billets at 0856 hours. Route :– BERSILLIES – VILLERS SUR NICOLAI along BAVAI – BINCHE Road to ESTINNE AU MONT, arriving in billets at 1455 hours. Batt H.Q. established at NO 12, RUE TRIEUX. Afternoon spent in cleaning up and foot inspections, etc.	MWH

A5234 Wt.W4973/M687 730,000 8/16 D.D.& L. Ltd. Forms/C2118/13.

WAR DIARY or INTELLIGENCE SUMMARY

Army Form C. 2118.

SHEET 3.

1/8TH LANCASHIRE FUSILIERS

Place	Date 1918	Hour	Summary of Events and Information	Remarks and references to Appendices
Ref MAP Sheet NAMUR 81 S.E. 1/100,000	Nov 16		Battalion marched on to ANDERLUES, leaving billets at 0911 hours, passing through	O.O. 134.
ESTINNES-AU-MONT			BINCE along MONS-CHARLEROI road, arriving in billets at ANDERLUES at 1245hrs.	
			The billets being widely scattered along the RUE MARAIS it was decided to billet A & B	MAH.
			Coys in the town in the RUE CHARBONIERE and PLACE de TEU BALLE. Bat.H.Q. established	
			at 37 RUE MARAIS. The afternoon was spent in cleaning of equipment, foot inspections.	
ANDERLUES	17		C & D Coys vacated their billets in the S area of RUE MARAIS at 1000 hrs and moved	O.O. 134.
			into the town along the RUE NIVELLE. The battalion was occupied throughout the	
			day in cleaning etc, interrupting its moving into CHARLEROI during the morning.	
			The GOC 42nd Div. visited the Battalion to present Lt Smith G. 524271 "B" Coy with	MAH.
			a watch.	
"	18		The Battalion moved on to CHARLEROI, leaving ANDERLUES at 0915 hrs, marching	O.O. 134.
			by main MONS road, arriving at the Infantry Barracks, CHARLEROI at 1300 hrs, occupying	
			the SOUTHERN WING. Afternoon was spent in organisation and cleaning of new quarters	
			Latrines, washhouses etc. Heavy rain lasted throughout the day.	MAH.
CHARLEROI	19		The day was spent in general cleaning up of the barracks, establishment of	MAH.
			dining rooms, washhouses etc. Men were instructed in methods of laying out hot	

WAR DIARY
or
INTELLIGENCE SUMMARY.
(Erase heading not required.)

Army Form C. 2118.

SHEET 4.
1/8th LANCASHIRE FUSILIERS

Place	Date	Hour	Summary of Events and Information	Remarks and references to Appendices
NAMURS ROAD CAMP CHARLEROI	20		Conferences were at the Defence of O.C. Companies. Training in P.T. & B. & Close order Drill, Polishing, Musketry, Training etc were carried out on the Battn Parade Ground.	W.G.
—	21		The day was devoted to bathing, cleaning & general re-distribution of barrack rooms.	W.G.
—	22	9.45	Church Parade — held in Museum Room of University or Turnhout Boulevard Colony.	W.G.
—	23		Training was carried out in Section, Squad & Coy Drill. The afternoon was devoted to decorating the men's dining hall for X'mas.	W.G.
—	24	9.30	C.O.'s Parade. Inspection of King's Regimental Colour. After this Parade the remainder of the morning was spent in Regimental Training — Formation of the wounded.	W.G.
—	25	10.00	Voluntary Church Parade held in Coliseum Theatre Boulevard Audent. The Brigadier General inspected the decorated dining halls of the Battn. General Holiday.	W.G.
—	26			W.G.

WAR DIARY
INTELLIGENCE SUMMARY. SHEET 5

1/8 LANCASHIRE FUSILIERS

Army Form C. 2118.

Place	Date	Hour	Summary of Events and Information	Remarks and references to Appendices
NAMUR ¥100,000 CHARLEROI	27	9.30	Training was carried out with Lewis & mr. Pelton [Section Drill] Battn. football Range formed (1 team for Co). The afternoon was devoted to Company football match.	W.C.
—	28	9.0	Advanced Class commenced. 3/8 O.R's from Coy attended lectures on Reconstruction by Mr Purdom at Eden Theatre Boulevard Jeanne Bertrand. The afternoon was devoted to Sport.	W.C.
—	29	10.30	Church Parade. Service held in Rollin Theatre Boulevard Audent W. Battn Kit Inspection.	W.C.
—	30	09.00	"A" Company fired elementary musketry course on the range. No. 1 of Lewis gun teams fired a revolver practice B.C.D. Co. carried out Section Platoon Drill on Battn Parade Ground "C" & HQ Coy bathed. The afternoon was devoted to football.	W.C.
—	31	09.00	Functional Training. Close Order Drill A & B Co bathed. Battn. football match in afternoon.	W.C.

Cmdg. 1/8th Bn. Lancashire Fusiliers Reg.

Army Form C. 2118.

WAR DIARY
INTELLIGENCE SUMMARY
1/5th Bn LANCASHIRE FUSILIERS

SHEET 1

(Erase heading not required.)

Place	Date	Hour	Summary of Events and Information	Remarks and references to Appendices
Ref Map 1919 NAMUR 1/100,000 CHARLEROI	JAN 1	0930	The Batt: turned out Section & Platoon Training in the morning.	J.S. 24 AF
	2	0915	Commanding Officers fortnightly Parade Dress:- Rifle, Belt + Bayonet - Education of Batt: Gunners was carried on in the morning. Afternoon:- footbal match "B" Coy v "C" Coy. "A" "D" Coy Battled.	W.E.
	3		The morning was devoted to cleaning Gunners Coys instruction of Batt: Gunners. Battalion officers, the officers of the Batt: were photographed in the Barrack Square. Afternoon:- Football. "A" Coy v "D" Coy.	I.P.
	4	0915	The Batt: paraded for Batt: photograph in the Barrack square. All officers N.C.O's & men who came on active service with the Batt: were photographed. Route Marches & training in the morning. In the afternoon there was a football match "A" v "D" Church Parade:- Held at Eden Theatre Boulevard Audent.	M. W.E.
	5	1030		W.E.
	6	930	All men not detailed for Brigade Duties paraded for work on the range. In the afternoon there was a football match "C" v "D"	W.E.

WAR DIARY

INTELLIGENCE SUMMARY.

Sheet 2.
1/8 Lancashire Fusiliers

Army Form C. 2118.

(Erase heading not required.)

Instructions regarding War Diaries and Intelligence Summaries are contained in F. S. Regs., Part II. and the Staff Manual respectively. Title pages will be prepared in manuscript.

Place	Date 1919	Hour	Summary of Events and Information	Remarks and references to Appendices
NAMUR BELGIUM CHARLEROI	JAN 7	0930	All men not detailed for Educational Classes paraded for work on the range. fini-8th 'D' Co. listed. The afternoon was devoted to football 'A' v 'B'.	WC
—	8	0900	A & B Co. carried out training in Physical section. Platoon relieved drill on the Batt. Parade Ground. 'D' Co. proceeded to work on the Range. 'B' & 'A' Co. listed.	WC
—	9	0900 11.45	Educational training. 1 Officer & 30 or's per company attended a lecture on Conveyancing at the Eden Theatre.	WC
—	10	0900	'D' Co. to mount Batt. Guard. All men not detailed for duties proceeded to Range. Work was completely fine throughout. Educational training was carried out in the morning.	WC
—	11	0900	Men not attending classes were employed cleaning out Commanding Officers inspection of Barracks.	WC
—	12	10.00	Church Parade. Service in Eden Theatre.	WC AC
—	13	9.0	'B' Co. first ground practice on the range. 'A' C & D Co. carried out training under Company arrangements.	WC

Army Form C. 2118.

WAR DIARY
or
INTELLIGENCE SUMMARY.
(Erase heading not required.)

SHEET 3

1/8th Bn LANCASHIRE FUSILIERS.

Place	Date	Hour	Summary of Events and Information	Remarks and references to Appendices
REF MAP 1915 NAMUR & CHARLEROI	JAN 1919 14	09.00	Educational Training was carried out in the morning all men not actually attending lectures engaged on the range. Thereafter was devoted to football. Bn played 1/7 L.F.	
	15		The Bn. bathed in the morning.	
	16		Educational Training was carried out in the morning. One Officer and 39 no. o.r. attended a lecture in the Nivelles Theatre on "The Naval Raid on Zeebrugge".	
	17		The men who marched to the Nivelles Barracks — the Bn paraded 6/Yorks. Rgt. for inspection of the hands at 12.00. Bn paraded and 30 o. attended a lecture at the Nivelles Theatre and 30 o. attended a lecture at the Nivelles Theatre on "Empire Emigration". One officer and 30 o.r. attended a lecture at the Nivelles Theatre on "British Empire Emigration".	
	18		The Divisional Commander Brigadier General Rettens to inspect "A" Coy (Sgt.) the Brigade Paraded on the "Place de Marquerend". The band played Regton attended a lecture by the American Senator at 12.00. Lecturer Smythington Pronouncing Bruno Parade Held in Sibon "Eden Theatre".	
	19			
	20		Coys were at the disposal of Coy Commanders for Games. One Officer and 30 o.r. per Bn. not attending the Games, marched to Namur. Heros. Officers visit the Army sports.	

WAR DIARY or INTELLIGENCE SUMMARY

Army Form C. 2118.

SHEET 4

Place	Date	Hour	Summary of Events and Information	Remarks and references to Appendices
NAMUR	JAN. 21		Educational classes and games met in the morning. All men not on duty or on fatigues were given training on the Ranges.	
MARLERUN	22		One company carried out Open Musketry on the Ranges. Remainder Coys went to Baths.	
	23		The commanding officer inspected the Battn on parade at 1 p.m. After this Parade Educational Training was carried out.	
	24		6 O.R's. 12 J.R's. to hospital. The Battn on parade. The Battn monitored training, during the morning. Officers & Educational Training.	
	25		Parade diverted to Educational Games & Baths. One Officer and 30 men on Coy attended a lecture on the Rheims Situation at 12 noon. Lecture interesting.	
	26		Officer's lecture on the Eden Society.	
	27		Gardener were at the disposal of the Coys for training during the morning.	
	28		Parade diverted to Educational Training.	
	29		Parade diverted to Engines Baths.	
	30		" Educational games in the Rays.	
	31		Coy on carried out Arms Practice on the Ranges. Remainder Coy's under Coy Commanders for training	

CONFIDENTIAL

WAR DIARY

OF

1/8th LANCASHIRE FUSILIERS

FROM 1/2/19 TO 28/2/19

VOLUME 46

1/8TH BATTALION,
LANCASHIRE FUSLS.

WAR DIARY
or
INTELLIGENCE SUMMARY.
(Erase heading not required.)

1/8th Bn LANCASHIRE FUSILIERS.

SHEET 1

Instructions regarding War Diaries and Intelligence Summaries are contained in F.S. Regs., Part II. and the Staff Manual respectively. Title pages will be prepared in manuscript.

Place	Date	Hour	Summary of Events and Information	Remarks and references to Appendices
NAMUR 1/100000 CHARLEROI.	FEB. 1		Educational Training was carried out in the morning. The Bath battles	DG
	2	1030	Church Parade held in Roden Theatre	DG
	3		Companies were at the disposal of Company Commanders for training	DG
	4		Educational Training	DG
	5		Companies were at the disposal of Company Commanders	DG
	6	1000	Commanding Officers parade. Dress:- Clean fatigue Educational Training was carried out	DG
	7		Companies at disposal of Company Commanders Educational Training	DG
	8		Church parade held in Roden Theatre	DG
	9	1030	Companies at disposal of Company Commanders Educational Training	DG
	10		Companies at disposal of Company Commanders Educational Training	DG
	11		Companies at disposal of Company Commanders, Batt: bathed	DG
	12		Educational Training	DG
	13		Companies at disposal of Company Commanders	DG
	14		Bn. left Infantry Barracks & gave over Cavalry Barracks	DG

WAR DIARY
or
INTELLIGENCE SUMMARY.

Army Form C. 2118.

SHEET II
1/8 Bn LANCASHIRE FUSILIERS

Place	Date	Hour	Summary of Events and Information	Remarks and references to Appendices
NAMUR 5100.000 SHEET 101	FEB 15		All available men were employed cleaning Barracks which were vacated by the Belgian Infantry Church Parade. Held in Billet Theatre.	
	16	10.30		
	17		All available men were employed cleaning Barracks. Educational Training in progress. All men not detailed for Educational Training were employed Cleaning Barracks.	
	18			
	19		Educational Training.	
	20		Companies at Disposal of Coy. Comdrs.	
	21		Educational Training. Battalion	
	22		Church Parade held in Eden Centre	
	23			
	24		Barrack Fatigue	
	25		Battalion Football	
	26		Battalion Football	
	27		Barrack Fatigues	
	28		do	

James S. MacLeod Major
1/8 Lancashire Fusiliers.

WAR DIARY or INTELLIGENCE SUMMARY

Army Form C. 2118.

SHEET 1

1/8th Bn LANCASHIRE FUSILIERS.

Place	Date	Hour	Summary of Events and Information	Remarks and references to Appendices
NAMUR	March 1		Conference at Disposal of Coy Comrs	
TODDOO	2		do	
CHARLEROI	3		do	
	4			
	5			
	6		The Battn. httled	
	7		All available men were employed cleaning barracks	
	8		The Battn. hatted. Medicine inspection in Barrack Room. They were billeted in the Cavalry Barracks. Received 50 P.O.W.	
	9	10.30	Church Parade held in Eden Theatre	
	10	10.30	The Cine and Draft for 15th-16th Lance Fus: were inspected. Drew - Marching order - the Battn. hatted	
	11		Conference at Disposal of Coy Comrs	
	12		All available men were employed cleaning Barracks, the Battn. is now down to cadre strength after leaving the duties connected of P.O.W. guard, instruction of drafts etc	
	13			
	14			
	15		Conference at Disposal of Coy Comrs	
	16		Church Parade held in Eden Theatre	
	17		C.O's inspection of drafts leaving	
	18	11.00	Conference at disposal of Coy Comrs. First Coy's marched off to entrain to Command 150 Infantry Brigade	

45 N

WAR DIARY or INTELLIGENCE SUMMARY.

Army Form C. 2118.

SHEET 2

1/6 LANCASHIRE FUSILIERS

Place	Date	Hour	Summary of Events and Information	Remarks and references to Appendices
REF MAP NAMUR 1/100000 CHARLEROI 1/200000	MARCH 19 20		The Batt moved to JESUIT COLLEGE. The Batt was employed cleaning vacated Cavalry Barracks. These Batt. quarters.	
	21		men were employed cleaning & whitewashing rooms in present college.	
	22	10.30	Continued internal of Coy Courses.	
	23	10.30	C.O's inspection of Coys. Church Parade held in open Theatre. Clothing exchange parade for men in Cadre strength Companies at disposal of Coy Comdrs.	
	24		do	
	25		The Batt loitered	
	26		The cadre made preparations for entraining on	
	27		the 29/3/19	
	28		Men sent in groups where the Cadre left in Ireland via Antwerp.	
	29			

A copiós

www.ingramcontent.com/pod-product-compliance
Lightning Source LLC
Chambersburg PA
CBHW081530160426
43191CB00011B/1723